Dear Mrs. Murphy

Thank you for a terrific year in Science class. We had a lot of fun. We will miss you. Good luck in your new school

Love,
Chris,
Meghan,
and
Kaitlin

QUIET MOMENTS
WITH GOD
FOR TEACHERS

HONOR
BOOKS

07 06 05 04 03   10 9 8 7 6 5 4 3 2 1

Quiet Moments with God for Teachers
ISBN 1-56292-689-6
Copyright © 2003 by Honor Books
An Imprint of Cook Communications Ministries
P.O. Box 55388
Tulsa, Oklahoma 74155

INTRODUCTION

The day starts loud and early even before the first bell rings. The end of the day is even louder, with your students racing out the door for home. What would you give for just a few moments of quiet?

Here is an invitation to your own "quiet break," taken whenever you want. A few moments spent inside these pages can help bring peace to your soul, helping you through even the most difficult of days. Quiet moments are not optional—you must set aside one-on-one time with God daily in order to get to know Him and be refreshed in His grace and peace. Without these times alone, you will become a slave to your lesson plans and school calendar.

We hope you will find the stories and encouragement you hold in your hands to be helpful and thought provoking. We have selected those that relate best to the everyday challenges of a teacher. They are short enough to fit easily into your special time with God, yet long enough to provide a lift during your day. As you read, it is our prayer that you are drawn into a more intimate relationship with our loving Father.

STAYING CHARGED UP

The age we live in has been described as the age of the to-do list that can't be done. Facing overwhelming demands, it's hard to give ourselves permission to rest or take a break. But the rewards—renewed perspective, clearer insight, physical energy, spiritual preparedness—are well worth it.

Before automatic headlight controls were installed in automobiles, it was easy to park a car and leave the headlights on. Perhaps we were in a hurry or it was light enough outside that we forgot we had turned on the lights. If we were gone for very long, we returned to find the car battery dead. To get the car running again, the battery had to be recharged.

Just like a car battery, our own supply of energy is not infinite. We must replenish it frequently with sleep, rest, food, and relaxation. Our busy nonstop days can be draining. Operating at top speed, we utilize all available emotional, physical, mental, and spiritual resources. Before we know it, our energy is consumed.

LET THE PEOPLE RENEW THEIR STRENGTH.

ISAIAH 41:1 KJV

Unless we pay careful attention, we will drain our "batteries" to the point of feeling "dead on our feet." Being fatigued can cause our perceptions to be distorted and our responses to others to be negative. Furthermore, if we fail to do something about it, over time it can result in physical or emotional illness.

Charles Spurgeon, a well-known nineteenth-century preacher said, "Without constant restoration we are not ready for the perpetual assaults. If we allow the good in our lives to get weak—or our 'light' to grow dim—the evil will surely gather strength and struggle desperately for the mastery over us."

You are wise to take a short break now and then during the day—and to turn off your lights when you go to bed at night! Living this way will help you to maintain your energy supply and enable you to be more productive and content.

TAKE REST; A FIELD THAT HAS
RESTED GIVES A BOUNTIFUL CROP.

OVID

USE THAT POWERFUL ENGINE!

What a pleasure it is to drive a car with a powerful engine on a level highway. Picture a sunny day when there's no traffic and you're not in a hurry to get anywhere. You sing along with your favorite CD and enjoy driving solely for driving's sake.

We are more likely to find ourselves in a much less powerful vehicle, however, climbing a series of steep hills in the rain with lots of traffic behind us and in front of us—and late for school.

But is it possible to ride the rougher road and have the same peace and tranquillity inside as when we drive the level highway? The Bible says it is.

The difference is simply the powerful engine, which makes the hills seem less steep and rush hour less tedious. It's a lot easier to keep moving steadily through traffic when you have a continuous hum from the motor, instead of lurching, dying, starting—lurching, dying, starting—in your own strength.

God is our powerful engine. He makes the difficult highway become manageable.

Perhaps your day started out smoothly, but by now you've left the easy stretch of road and come to the rolling hills. Now more than ever is the time to remind yourself that your Father in Heaven loves you and wants to help you.

With God's strength, you can stay alert and focused, maintaining an even pace and an even temperament regardless of the challenge. Ask Him, and He will help you work through any problems that arise without compromising your integrity. He may even show you some shortcuts—and the gas mileage is great!

WHEN A MAN HAS NO
STRENGTH, IF HE LEANS
ON GOD, HE BECOMES
POWERFUL.

DWIGHT LYMAN MOODY

FAULTY ASSUMPTIONS

Anita went to the teacher's lounge and bought a small package of cookies to eat while grading papers. Gradually, she became aware of a rustling noise. Looking up from her papers, she was flabbergasted to see one of the other teachers helping himself to her cookies. Not wanting to make a scene, she leaned over and took a cookie herself.

A minute or two passed, and then she heard more rustling. He was helping himself to another cookie! By this time, they had come to the end of the package. She was angry but didn't dare allow herself to say anything. Then, as if to add insult to injury, the man broke the remaining cookie in two, pushed half across to her, ate the other half, and left.

Still fuming later when it was time to return to class, Anita picked up her things. To her shock and embarrassment, there was her pack of unopened cookies!

THE PRIDE OF THINE HEART HATH DECEIVED THEE, THOU THAT DWELLEST IN THE CLEFTS OF THE ROCK, WHOSE HABITATION IS HIGH; THAT SAITH IN HIS HEART, WHO SHALL BRING ME DOWN TO THE GROUND?

OBADIAH 1:3 KJV

It's so easy to make assumptions about what is happening around us. We expect things to be a certain way based on past experience, what we know, or what we have been told about a situation. Assumptions are not always wrong, but they are never to be trusted. Too many times they lead to embarrassment and even destruction.

The Bible tells us that assumption is based on human reasoning, and the driving force behind it is pride. As the verse above says, it is pride—thinking we know everything—which allows us to be deceived.

Pride caused Anita to assume she was right and the other teacher was wrong. Instead of seeing him through God's eyes and praying for wisdom to handle the situation God's way, she ignored the man. In the end, she was completely blind to his kindness toward her.

Try to see other people and situations through God's eyes. After all, your vision is limited, but He knows exactly what's going on!

IT IS OUR OWN EGO THAT
MAKES THE EGO OF OTHERS
INTOLERABLE TO US.

FRANÇOIS DUC DE LA ROCHEFOUCAULD

The Spice of Life

Most of us have a routine we follow every morning. There's also a certain routine for our jobs and another one that takes over after work. Even on the weekends, there are things that must be done.

Have you come to dread another stack of papers to grade, another test to prepare, or another conference to attend? Is there any end to the "routine" of life?

BECAUSE OF THE LORD'S GREAT LOVE WE ARE NOT CONSUMED, FOR HIS COMPASSIONS NEVER FAIL. THEY ARE NEW EVERY MORNING; GREAT IS YOUR FAITHFULNESS.

LAMENTATIONS 3:22-23

There's no getting out of most of those tasks. Someone has to keep things running smoothly. The one thing we *can* control is our attitude toward it all.

Rather than emphasizing the "same old," we should remember what the Bible says: "If anyone is in Christ, he is a new creation; the old has gone, the new has come!" (2 Corinthians 5:17), and "I will give you a new heart and put a new spirit in you" (Ezekiel 36:26).

God never changes, but He loves variety. He wants us to embrace life and keep our eyes open for new possibilities, our minds open to new ideas, our hearts open to new people who cross our path.

Even in the midst of the "same old same old" daily routine, He can bring something new, unusual, and different. Sometimes upsetting the routine can be distressing. But don't let it shake your confidence in God's plan for your life; let it enhance His plan.

Today, be aware that whether life seems to have a "sameness" or has turned chaotic, you are always changing inside. Through it all, the Lord is continually stirring new life within you, giving you new dreams and goals, and molding you to be more like Jesus each day!

LET NOTHING DISTURB THEE,

LET NOTHING AFFRIGHT THEE.

ALL THINGS ARE PASSING.

GOD NEVER CHANGES.

PATIENCE GAINS ALL THINGS.

WHO HAS GOD WANTS NOTHING.

GOD ALONE SUFFICES.

SAINT TERESA OF AVILA

THE CELEBRITY GARDEN

I AM A ROSE OF SHARON. . . .
LIKE A LILY AMONG THORNS IS MY
DARLING AMONG THE MAIDENS.

SONG OF SONGS 2:1-2

Sherry had finally cleaned a spot in her backyard for a rose garden—her dream for many years. As she thumbed through a rose catalog, she sighed at the magnitude of her choices. *Just like a Christmas wish list,* she thought. *Which ones should I pick? A white John F. Kennedy; a large, pink Peggy Lee; a red Mr. Lincoln; the delicate Queen Elizabeth rose?*

Sherry closed her eyes as if in deep thought. Suddenly, she had an idea, *I'll plant my own celebrity garden.*

The next day Sherry hurried to her local nursery and bought a dozen roses—all colors and sizes. She worked hard that week, carefully planting each rose. Finally, her task was done, and she decided to throw a party and invite all her friends to help her celebrate her celebrity rose garden.

Imagine their surprise when her friends watched Sherry unveil the celebrity names she had placed on each rose. One by one, they read their own names beside the flowers. The celebrities in Sherry's garden were none other than her friends. But in the middle of the fragrant bouquet, one rose still remained a mystery.

She unveiled the label, which read, "Rose of Sharon." "This One is the love of my life, and everything else centers around Him."

A thousand "celebrities" cry out for our time and attention. Relationships, like a healthy garden, need ample doses of love and affirmation. When Christ is at the center of our affection, all other loves will fall into place.

In the garden of your life, who are your celebrities?

THE ORNAMENTS OF
OUR HOUSE ARE
THE FRIENDS WHO
FREQUENT IT.

RALPH WALDO EMERSON

WITH ATTITUDE

"To love what you do and feel that it matters—how could anything be more fun?" asks Katharine Graham. That's what we all desire, isn't it?

No matter what work we do, our attitude toward our work is vital to our basic sense of self-worth. The ideal for us all is to love the work we do and feel that it has significance. While no job is enjoyable or pleasant all the time, it is possible to derive satisfaction from what we bring to a job—the attitude with which we perform our tasks.

WHATEVER YOU DO, DO ALL TO THE GLORY OF GOD.

1 CORINTHIANS 10:31 RSV

Brother Lawrence, the seventeenth-century Carmelite, found joy in his job washing dishes at the monastery. In the monotony of his routine work, he found the opportunity to focus on God and feel His presence.

Modern-day entrepreneurs Ben Cohen and Jerry Greenfield make and sell ice cream with a purpose. The bottom line of Ben & Jerry's Homemade Inc. is "How much money is left over at the end of the year?" and "How have we improved life in the community?"

"Leftover money" goes to fund the Ben & Jerry's Foundation, which distributes funds to worthy nonprofit causes. These are charities that help needy children, preserve the Amazonian rain forest, provide safe shelter for emotionally or psychologically distressed people, and fund a business staffed by formerly unemployed homeless people. By helping others with their profits, Ben and Jerry put more *meaning* into their ice cream business.

The Scriptures teach that all service ranks the same with God, because it is not *what* you do that matters, but the *spirit* in which you do it. A street sweeper who does his work to serve God and bless the people who travel on the streets is as pleasing to Him as the priest or pastor who teaches and nurtures his congregation.

If you feel your work is insignificant, ask God to open your eyes! When you do all for Him and to serve others, no task is unimportant!

EVERY GIFT WHICH IS GIVEN,
EVEN THOUGH IT BE SMALL, IS
GREAT IF GIVEN WITH AFFECTION.

PINDAR

HOLY HUMOR

Is laughter theologically correct? We rarely think of a knee-slapping, rib-tickling, belly laugh when we think of being spiritual. But is that God's perspective?

In Umberto Eco's novel *The Name of the Rose,* a villainous monk named Jorge poisoned anyone who came upon the one book in the monastery library that suggested that God laughed. Jorge feared if the monks thought God laughed, He would become too familiar to them, too common, and they would lose their awe of Him. Jorge probably never considered the idea that laughter is one of the things that sets us apart as made in God's image.

In *Spiritual Fitness,* Doris Donnelly tells us that humor has two elements: an acceptance of life's incongruities and the ability not to take ourselves too seriously. The Christian faith is filled with incongruities—the meek inherit the earth, the simple teach wisdom, death leads to life, a virgin gives birth, a King is born in a stable. Many, but not all, of life's incongruities are humorous.[1]

Humor also helps us let go of an exaggerated sense of importance

> HE WHO SITS IN
> THE HEAVENS
> SHALL LAUGH.
>
> PSALM 2:4 NKJV

and face the truth about ourselves. Anxiety over our own efforts can obscure what God is doing in our lives. "Lighten up" can be good spiritual advice!

How can we renew our sense of humor?

- Be on the lookout for humor. Almost every situation contains some element of humor.

- Spend time with people who have a sense of humor—their perspective will be contagious.

- Practice laughing. Take a five- to ten-minute laugh break every day.

You can benefit from laughing. Humor requires a sense of honesty about yourself—without arrogance or false humility. Humor has also been proven to be good for your health. Take time to laugh each day—it is good for the soul as well as the body.

ONE IS SCARCELY AWARE OF FATIGUE
WHILE HE MARCHES TO MUSIC.

THOMAS CARLYLE

A PARTY FOR JESUS

"TRUE WORSHIPERS WILL WORSHIP
THE FATHER IN SPIRIT AND TRUTH."

JOHN 4:23

How would you feel if a party was given in your honor and the people attending gave presents to one another but not to you?

That's the question Mable Dumas addressed at her prayer group's monthy meeting. As the ladies arrived in her home, she served refreshments and then said, "Ladies, we like to visit with one another, but from this point on, let's talk only about Jesus. He is our guest of honor this evening."

As the women gathered around the fireplace, Mable sat on the hearth and led a conversation about Jesus. The focal point became a wooden cross.

The ladies discussed everything from Jesus' humble birth to His death and resurrection.

Then Mable announced, "Every party has gifts. Now it's our time for us to give our gifts to Jesus." She passed around a basket filled with tiny, decorated boxes. At the appointed time, each participant opened her box in an attitude of prayer and read aloud a Scripture, along with the companion "gift" to place on an altar. These included such things as:

- my heart
- my faith
- my future
- my dreams

During the touching, intimate moment, several women moved to a kneeling position and then wept softly. That day became special, because the ladies chose to give Jesus the most meaningful gift of all: *themselves*.

IN WORSHIP WE MEET
THE POWER OF GOD AND
IN ITS STRENGTHENING.

NELS F. S. FERRÉ

WHAT DO YOU KNOW?

"**K**nowledge is of two kinds," said Samuel Johnson. "We know a subject ourselves, or we know where we can find information upon it."

There's also a third area of knowledge: the *unknowable*. Try as we might to uncover all the secrets of the universe, there are simply some things we will never discover or comprehend. As the apostle Paul told the Corinthians, "Now I know in part; then [in the afterlife] I shall know fully, even as I am fully known" (1 Corinthians 13:12).

It's tempting to become a know-it-all. Knowing how to do something, how to fix something, how to find something, gives us a good feeling. We have all experienced the rewards associated with learning new skills and developing them to the best of our ability.

Most of us also enjoy having others turn to us for answers or information. Much of our self-esteem is derived from what we know and what we can do.

But there must be a balance. We must face the hard fact that we can never know everything there is to know

> I CONSIDER EVERYTHING A LOSS COMPARED TO THE SURPASSING GREATNESS OF KNOWING CHRIST JESUS MY LORD.
>
> PHILIPPIANS 3:8

about anything. We can never achieve perfection of skill to the point where we never make mistakes. In fact, the more we know about something, the more we realize how much we *don't* know. The more proficient our skills, the more we are aware that accidents happen, some days are "off" days, and everyone has a slump now and then.

If we choose, we can become obsessed with our own perfection and potential, spending all our available time reading and studying and taking courses. We might listen to teaching tapes while we jog and make every vacation "a learning experience."

A wiser approach to life, however, is to spend more time knowing God. The more you know Him, the easier it is to trust Him, hear His voice, and show His love to your students, family, friends, neighbors, and coworkers. You will learn the things you will need to know in order to do His will. What we know and can do is never as satisfying or meaningful as knowing God and serving others.

ALL WE KNOW IS STILL
INFINITELY LESS THAN ALL
THAT STILL REMAINS UNKNOWN.

WILLIAM HARVEY

WINDOW ON THE WORLD

A story from England called *The Wonderful Window* tells about a London clerk who worked in drab and depressing circumstances. His office building was in a rundown part of the city and had not been maintained.

But that ordinary clerk was not about to let his outlook on life be determined by the dreariness of his surroundings. So one day he bought a beautiful, multi-colored Oriental window painted with an inspiring scene.

The clerk took his window to his workplace and had it installed high on the wall in his office. When the hardworking, dispirited clerk looked through his window, he did not see the familiar slum scenes, with dark streets and dirty marketplaces. Instead he saw a fair city with beautiful castles and towers, green parks, and lovely homes on wide tree-lined streets. On the highest tower of the window there was a large white banner with a strong knight protecting the fair city from a fierce and dangerous dragon. This wonderful window put a "halo" on the everyday tasks of the young man.

Somehow as he worked long hours at tedious book work and

O LORD, I PRAY,

OPEN HIS EYES

THAT HE MAY SEE.

2 KINGS 6:17 NASB

accounting, trying to make everything balance, he felt he was working for that knight on the banner. This feeling produced a sense of honor and dignity. He had found a noble purpose helping the knight keep the city happy, beautiful, prosperous, and strong.

You don't have to let your circumstances or surroundings discourage you, either. God has sent you to your school to do noble work for Him. You are His teacher, bringing His beauty to everyone around you.

NO ONE EVER ATTAINS VERY EMINENT SUCCESS BY SIMPLY DOING WHAT IS REQUIRED OF HIM; IT IS THE AMOUNT AND EXCELLENCE OF WHAT IS OVER AND ABOVE THE REQUIRED THAT DETERMINES THE GREATNESS OF ULTIMATE DISTINCTION.

CHARLES KENDALL ADAMS

THE TROUBLE WITH BEING RIGHT

Believe it or not, it's often harder to gracefully receive an apology than it is to issue one. As Christians, we know we are to forgive "seventy times seven" times (Matthew 18:22 KJV), but some of us can sincerely forgive and still project an air of superiority unbecoming to a child of the King.

If you're waiting for someone to realize they owe you an apology, take time to think of a response that reflects genuine forgiveness and allows the transgressor to feel he or she has retained your respect. Consider this humorous little story:

A passenger on a dining car looked over the luncheon menu. The list included both a chicken salad sandwich and a chicken sandwich. He decided on the chicken salad sandwich but absentmindedly wrote chicken sandwich on the order slip. When the waiter brought the chicken sandwich, the customer angrily protested.

Most waiters would have immediately picked up the order slip and shown the customer the mistake was his. This waiter didn't. Instead, expressing regret at the error, he picked up the chicken sandwich, returned to the kitchen, and a moment later placed a chicken salad sandwich in front of the customer.

While eating his sandwich, the customer picked up the order slip and saw that the mistake had been his. When it came time to pay the check, the man apologized to the waiter and offered to pay for both sandwiches. The waiter's response was, "No, sir. That's perfectly all right. I'm just happy you've forgiven me for being right."

Next time someone blames you for their mistake, don't get defensive, but find a creative way to make things right.

AS WE GROW IN WISDOM,

WE PARDON MORE FREELY.

ANNE-LOUISE-GERMAINE DE STAËL

SPONTANEOUS LOVE BOUQUETS

Melanie read the suggestions carefully. "Place contrasting colors together, like peach with blue. Or try red, white, and blue, for a bright, patriotic flower bed. If you prefer, naturalize your bulbs, incorporating them into your yard's natural habitat. This works particularly well if you live in a wooded, grassy area."

She grabbed her gardener's tools and set to work, planting some in circles and others in rows. Melanie reserved a handful of varied size bulbs, and like a mother hiding Easter eggs for her expectant child, she tossed bulbs randomly on the grass. Wherever they landed, Melanie carved a hole and dropped them in the ground.

Weeks passed, and Melanie forgot about the bulbs—including their secret hiding places. One early spring day, Melanie walked out in her backyard and saw green shoots poking through

> "DO NOT LET YOUR LEFT HAND KNOW WHAT YOUR RIGHT HAND IS DOING, SO THAT YOUR GIVING MAY BE IN SECRET. THEN YOUR FATHER, WHO SEES WHAT IS DONE IN SECRET, WILL REWARD YOU."
>
> MATTHEW 6:3-4

the earth. In the next few weeks, her yard looked like a magical wonderland. As she strolled through the green terrain, she realized the most fun part was seeing the bulbs pop up among the natural setting—beside trees, in the middle of a grassy slope, or tucked away in a corner. Nature had worked its magic and rewarded Melanie's long-forgotten efforts with a harvest of beautiful flowers.

Christlike deeds are like the bulbs in Melanie's garden. Some we plant in deliberate, orderly fashion. Others, because of the God-nature planted within us, spill out from our lives naturally like spontaneous love gifts to those around us. These colorful bouquets spring up in the most unexpected places, a true "God-thing," blessing us—and others—in a most beautiful way.

A BIT OF FRAGRANCE ALWAYS CLINGS
TO THE HAND THAT GIVES YOU ROSES.

CHINESE PROVERB

ACCEPTING SUBSTITUTES

A recently married woman moved to a small town in Wyoming. Clothing stores were in short supply, and her busy ranch life left little time for the long trips to larger cities to shop. Her situation was made more difficult by the fact that she was a hard-to-fit size. To solve her problem, she began relying on a major store catalog that carried her size. The printed order forms sent by the store had this sentence at the bottom: "If we do not have the article you ordered in stock, may we substitute?"

Since she rarely ordered unless she really needed the article in question, she was hesitant to trust strangers to make an appropriate substitution, but she replied yes, hoping it wouldn't be necessary.

This approach worked well until one day she opened a package from the company and found a letter which read, in part, "We are sorry that the article you ordered is out of stock, but we have substituted . . ." When she unwrapped the merchandise she found an article of greater quality worth double the price she had paid!

UNTO HIM THAT IS ABLE TO DO EXCEEDING ABUNDANTLY ABOVE ALL THAT WE ASK OR THINK, ACCORDING TO THE POWER THAT WORKETH IN US.

EPHESIANS 3:20 KJV

On each order after that, the woman wrote *yes* in large red letters at the bottom of the order form by the substitution question. She had confidence the store would provide her with the best they had to fill her order.

When we pray to God, we are wise to add to our requests that we are quite willing to accept a substitution for what we think we need. We can trust God to send us the perfect answer because, as our Maker, He knows what will fit us better than we do. Because He knows the future in a way that we do not, He can answer in a way that goes beyond our highest expectations. Every time He sends "substitutions," we can be sure He is sending something much better than we could have ever imagined.

BEWARE IN YOUR PRAYER, ABOVE EVERYTHING, OF LIMITING GOD, NOT ONLY BY UNBELIEF, BUT BY FANCYING THAT YOU KNOW WHAT HE CAN DO.

ANDREW MURRAY

WHO'S WATCHING?

THAT YE WOULD WALK WORTHY
OF GOD, WHO HATH CALLED YOU
UNTO HIS KINGDOM AND GLORY.

1 THESSALONIANS 2:12 KJV

Even though we are Christians, we can still live our lives and conduct our business like everyone else, right? After all, we are only human.

Wrong! Once we have accepted Jesus into our lives, we have the supernatural power of the Holy Spirit to help us be and do more than what is humanly possible. Even nonbelievers know that people who call themselves followers of Christ should operate differently than those who don't.

Take, for instance, this account of a man named Roy. He had been a kidnapper and holdup man for twelve years, but while in prison he heard the Gospel and invited Jesus Christ into his life: "Jesus said to me, 'I will come and live in you, and we will serve this sentence together.' And we did."

Several years later he was paroled, and just before he went out he was handed a two-page letter written by another prisoner, which said, "You know perfectly well that when I came into the jail, I despised preachers, the Bible, and anything that smacked of Christianity. I went to the Bible class and the preaching service because there wasn't anything else interesting to do.

"Then they told me you were saved, and I said, 'There's another fellow taking the Gospel road to get parole.' But, Roy, I've been watching you for two-and-a-half years. You didn't know it, but I watched you when you were in the yard exercising, when you were working in the shop, when you played, while we were all together at meals, on the way to our cells, and all over, and now I'm a Christian, too, because I watched you. The Saviour [sic] who saved you has saved me. You never made a slip."[2]

Who might be secretly watching you? A coworker, a child, a boss, or a spouse who needs to know Jesus? You are His representative to that person.

EXAMPLE IS THE MOST POWERFUL RHETORIC.

THOMAS BENTON BROOKS

UNCHANGING HOPE

No one knows for sure when ships were first used for water transportation. The earliest evidence of sailing vessels dates from Egypt about the third millennium BC. Since then, ships have changed considerably.

Today's passenger and cargo ships have no oars, sails, or masts. Modern vessels have all the conveniences of a great luxury hotel—gourmet cuisine, an array of entertainment, recreation, even swimming pools! One thing, however, has remained remarkably the same—the anchor. Except for the differing sizes, the anchor on Paul's ship of the first century and the anchor on the *Queen Elizabeth II* of the twentieth century are not much different.

> HE WILL NOT FEAR EVIL TIDINGS; HIS HEART IS STEADFAST, TRUSTING IN THE LORD.
>
> PSALM 112:7 NASB

The same could be said of human life. Technology has brought staggering changes in virtually every arena of our lives; however, people are still people. We experience the same struggles, temptations, joys, hopes, and sorrows of our ancestors—and our souls still need an anchor.

When Paul and his companions were shipwrecked on the coast of Malta, they dropped four anchors, which kept the ship from being dashed against the rocks. The writer of Hebrews tells us we have an anchor that will keep our lives from shipwreck—our hope in Jesus Christ.

Jesus keeps us safe and secure in the midst of storms and uncertainties. No matter what we face, because He is Lord of our lives, we have hope—hope for the future, hope to be healed, hope to succeed, hope to be free, hope to help others.

Just as no experienced sailor would go out to sea without an anchor, we must never go anywhere without Jesus![3]

BEHIND THE CLOUD THE STARLIGHT LURKS, THROUGH SHOWERS THE SUNBEAMS FALL; FOR GOD, WHO LOVETH ALL HIS WORKS HAS LEFT HIS HOPE WITH ALL!

JOHN GREENLEAF WHITTIER

ESCAPE VALVE

Have you just about had enough of that domineering coworker? Is your class out of control today? Are you tired of the attitude of that person you can't seem to avoid?

We all encounter people—sometimes on a frequent basis—that we just don't like. And to make matters worse, even those we do like can have a bad day!

Eleanor Roosevelt gave advice for that situation:

> BE MERCIFUL—
> SYMPATHETIC,
> TENDER,
> RESPONSIVE,
> AND COMPAS-
> SIONATE—EVEN
> AS YOUR FATHER
> IS [ALL THESE].
>
> LUKE 6:36 AMP

A mature person is one who does not think only in absolutes, who is able to be objective even when deeply stirred emotionally, who has learned that there is both good and bad in all people and in all things, and who walks humbly and deals charitably with the circumstances of life, knowing that in this world no one is all knowing and therefore all of us need both love and charity.

Certainly we would all like to attain such a level of maturity! But how? Jesus taught His followers in Luke 6:37 (AMP) there were three specific things they needed to do to get along with other people:

- Judge not—neither pronouncing judgment nor subjecting to censure—and you will not be judged.

- Do not condemn and pronounce guilty, and you will not be condemned and pronounced guilty.

- Acquit and forgive and release (give up resentment, let it drop), and you will be acquitted and forgiven and released.

Refuse to let another person put you in a pressure cooker today. Release the "steam" you feel by doing acts of kindness and praying.

ANGER IS QUIETED BY A GENTLE WORD
JUST AS FIRE IS QUENCHED BY WATER.

JEAN PIERRE CAMUS

THE RIPPLE EFFECT

[THE MUSTARD SEED] INDEED IS THE
LEAST OF ALL SEEDS: BUT WHEN IT IS
GROWN, IT IS THE GREATEST AMONG
HERBS, AND BECOMETH A TREE, SO
THAT THE BIRDS OF THE AIR COME AND
LODGE IN THE BRANCHES THEREOF.

MATTHEW 13:32 KJV

Not everyone who commits his or her life to Jesus
Christ will be called to be world famous. The majority
of us are called to fulfill less noticeable roles in our
churches, schools, communities, and families. Yet only
God may know how significant our roles are to the
future of thousands—even millions.

A century and a half ago a humble minister lived
and died in a small village in Leicestershire, England. He
lived there his entire life and never traveled far from
home. He never attended college, had no formal
degrees, but was a faithful village minister.

In his congregation was a young cobbler to whom
he gave special attention, teaching him the Word of
God. This young man was William Carey, later hailed as
one of the greatest missionaries of modern times.

The village minister also had a son—a boy whom he taught faithfully and constantly encouraged. The boy's character and talents were profoundly impacted by his father's life. That son grew up to be a man many considered the mightiest public orator of his day: Robert Hall. Widely admired for his saintly character, his preaching was powerful, and his sermons influenced the decisions of statesmen.

It seems the village pastor accomplished little in his life as a preacher. There were no spectacular revivals, great miracles, or major church growth. But his faithful witness and Godly life had much to do with giving India its Carey and England its Robert Hall.

When you think you are having no impact in the world, remember the little country preacher who influenced two nations for the Lord.

IF YOU WANT YOUR NEIGHBOR TO SEE WHAT CHRIST WILL DO FOR HIM, LET HIM SEE WHAT CHRIST HAS DONE FOR YOU.

HENRY WARD BEECHER

KEEP YOUR EYES ON HIM

Ginger ran to her mother's room as fast as her five-year-old legs would take her. "Come look; come quick," she squealed.

"What is it, honey?" her mother asked.

"You have to come see."

Ginger grabbed Mother by the hand and led her to the living room. Stopping in front of the credenza, Ginger pointed her chubby little finger to the manger scene.

When Mother had arranged the figures the previous night, the display was properly balanced and evenly spaced. The larger figures were near the stable, and the smaller ones were at the far edge of the walnut top so as to achieve proper perspective. Mother had been pleased with the visual picture. Now the figures were clustered under the stable roof. Each stood facing the manger, as close as possible to the Baby Jesus.

"Isn't that better? Now they can all see," Ginger proudly exclaimed.

"See?" asked her puzzled mother.

"Yes, see," said Ginger. "When I got up, all the men were scattered around. Some of them were so far away that they couldn't see Baby Jesus. I moved them closer, so they could see Him."

Can you see Jesus, or do you need to move a little closer to the manger in order to see the Savior?

BY A CARPENTER MANKIND WAS
MADE, AND ONLY BY THAT CARPENTER
CAN MANKIND BE REMADE.

DESIDERIUS ERASMUS

MORNING PRAISE!

A young school teacher moved away from her home to take a teaching position in New York City. She rented a room from an elderly lady who had migrated to the United States years before from Sweden. The landlady offered a clean room, a shared bathroom, and use of the kitchen at a reasonable rate.

The little white-haired Swedish woman made the rules of the house very clear. There would be no smoking or drinking, no food in the bedrooms, etc. Pausing mid-sentence, the landlady asked, "Do you sing? Do you play? Music is good! I used to play the piano at the church, but not now. I'm too old. My hearing isn't good, but I love to praise God with music. God loves music."

After a full day of moving into her new room, the young tenant slept soundly until 5:30 A.M. when she was jarred awake by horrible noises coming from somewhere downstairs. Cautiously making her way down the stairway, she followed the sounds to the kitchen door. There she discovered her new landlady standing at the stove, dressed for the day, joyfully "singing" at the top of her lungs!

COME BEFORE HIM WITH JOYFUL SINGING.

PSALM 100:2 NASB

Never had the young woman heard such a horrible voice. Yet

she heard that voice, precious to God, start every morning off the same way for as long as she rented the room just over the kitchen.

The Swedish lady passed into glory a few years later. The teacher moved on, married, and had her own family. She is alone now also and has lost some of her hearing. Yet, every morning finds her standing in front of the stove, singing off key and loud, but joyful, praises to the Lord!

A glorious way to start the day!

O FOR A THOUSAND TONGUES TO
SING MY GREAT REDEEMER'S PRAISE!

CHARLES WESLEY

GREAT BEGINNINGS

"LET YOUR LIGHT SO SHINE BEFORE MEN,
THAT THEY MAY SEE YOUR GOOD WORKS
AND GLORIFY YOUR FATHER IN HEAVEN."

MATTHEW 5:16 NKJV

In his best-seller, *The Seven Habits of Highly Effective People,* Stephen Covey titles one of the seven habits "Begin with the End in Mind." He uses an illustration of imagining yourself at your own funeral. If you close your eyes and imagine the people in attendance, the flowers, the music, and the minister delivering the eulogy, how would it go if your life were to end today?

How would you want it to be?

Through his illustration, Covey demonstrates that in order to achieve a goal, we must have that goal in mind in everything we do along the way.

More importantly, everything we do today—whether in line with our long-range desires or not—affects what we become for the rest of our lives. And what we become affects everyone whose lives we touch. What a ripple effect! There's an old Chinese proverb that says:

If there is light in the soul,
There will be beauty in the person.
If there is beauty in the person,
There will be harmony in the house.
If there is harmony in the house,
There will be order in the nation.
If there is order in the nation,
There will be peace in the world.

If you remember the 70s, you'll recognize the phrase, "Today is the first day of the rest of your life." Today is our opportunity to begin with the end in mind. If we begin with God's light in our souls, we can bring beauty, harmony, order, and peace—the Prince of Peace—to the world.

OUR PLANS MISCARRY
BECAUSE THEY HAVE NO
AIM. WHEN A MAN DOES
NOT KNOW WHAT HARBOR
HE IS MAKING FOR, NO
WIND IS THE RIGHT WIND.

LUCIUS ANNAEUS SENECA

THE INVITATION

Rita stood on the sidewalk, peering wistfully at the beautiful home. Through the curtained windows she saw nicely dressed people chatting with one another and enjoying refreshments. In her hand she clutched an engraved, personal invitation to the dinner party. She had been invited to attend this evening's affair by her professor, who was impressed with her academic abilities and wanted her to meet others at the university.

She carefully fingered the invitation, looked down at her nice "party dress," which seemed so dull and ordinary in comparison to the gowns she saw through the window, and with a sadness of the soul she turned and slowly walked away. Clutched between her fingers: the unused invitation.

> THE SON SAID UNTO HIM,
> FATHER, I . . .
> AM NO MORE
> WORTHY TO
> BE CALLED
> THY SON.
>
> LUKE 15:21 KJV

This poignant and painful scene from the British movie *Educating Rita* demonstrates just how difficult it is for one to accept the possibility of a new life. Rita came from a lower-middle-class family, and no one in her family had attended a university before her. She struggled with feelings of inadequacy and was forever wondering how she would "fit in." It is this sense of self-doubt that caused her to fail to take action on the invitation.

However, thanks to a persistent professor, who saw more in her than she saw in herself, she eventually accepted his invitation to join a new world. By the movie's end, this once modest woman excels as a scholar.

The invitation to become and then excel as a Christian is for each of us. The greatest joy, though, is in knowing that our Master Teacher always sees much more in us than we usually see in ourselves.

GOD DOES NOT ASK ABOUT OUR
ABILITY, BUT OUR AVAILABILITY.
GOD WANTS US TO BE VICTORS, NOT
VICTIMS; TO GROW, NOT GROVEL;
TO SOAR, NOT SINK; TO OVERCOME,
NOT TO BE OVERWHELMED.

WILLIAM ARTHUR WARD

THE MAGIC OF INSTRUCTIONS

Angrily the young man flung his wrench across the driveway and rolled away from the car. He had been trying for hours to change the brake pads on his wife's small foreign car. It didn't help matters that he was at best a mediocre mechanic. Finally, in exasperation he stormed into the house and informed his wife that something was seriously wrong with her car and he could not fix it.

"In fact," he shouted, "I don't know if anyone can fix it!"

She quietly thanked him for his efforts and then moved to the telephone where she called her father, a master mechanic. After she explained the situation, she and her father ventured to the nearest library where they found a manual for her car. They carefully made copies of the pages giving directions on how to change the brake pads. Next, they stopped at a foreign-car auto parts store and purchased a small but vital tool necessary for this particular job. Finally, they proceeded home

PAY ATTENTION AND LISTEN TO THE SAYINGS OF THE WISE.

PROVERBS 22:17

to her car, and within thirty minutes the repair job was complete.

What made the difference? Three things: first, she contacted her father, a master mechanic. The first instruction God gives us is to call upon Him. Second, they found the right set of instructions and carefully followed them. Sometimes we insist on trying to do things without consulting the instructions. Finally, they secured the proper tool to do the job. God will always give us the right tool if we will go and secure it.

Whether we are talking about brake pads or critical life decisions, it is simply amazing—almost magical—how well things work out when we follow the instructions.

A SINGLE CONVERSATION ACROSS THE TABLE WITH A WISE MAN IS WORTH A MONTH'S STUDY OF BOOKS.

AUTHOR UNKNOWN

OBEDIENCE AND PEACEFUL ABIDING

"ABIDE IN ME, AND I IN YOU."

JOHN 15:4 NASB

While on safari, a missionary family stopped for lunch. The children were playing under a tree a distance away from their parents and the other adults on the team. Suddenly the father of one child jumped up and yelled to his son, "Drop down!" and the son did so instantly. Others in the group were shocked to learn that a poisonous snake was slithering down the tree, ready to strike the child. It would have meant certain death if the snake had bitten him. Only the father of the child saw the snake.

Amazement was expressed over the instant response of the child to his father's command. The father explained the abiding love he and his son enjoyed had developed from the trust they had in each other. The boy did not question when his dad gave the command; he trusted him and responded accordingly. The missionary father also expected his son to respond to his command.

The peaceful rest that both of them were able to enjoy later that day was evidence of the abiding rest that

God has for each of us as we learn to trust Him. Are you abiding in Christ?

God wants to abide in us, and He wants us to abide in Him. Abiding comes more easily for some than others. It is not always easy to know what God has planned for us, but we can be assured that whatever it is, He is ready to equip us with what we need to endure and hold on to that place for as long as He wants us there. Abiding starts with trust and ends with complete rest.

ALL MY REQUESTS ARE LOST IN ONE, "FATHER, THY WILL BE DONE!"

CHARLES WESLEY

WHAT'S THE PROBLEM?

Ever had a difficulty that gives you "2:00 A.M. wake-up calls"? It could be a project at school, a committee you've suddenly ended up chairing, or simply trying to figure out how to get everything done with only two hands. Whatever the issue, it ruins your sleep and saps your energy for the upcoming day.

> I CAN DO
> ALL THINGS
> THROUGH
> CHRIST WHO
> STRENGTHENS
> ME.
>
> PHILIPPIANS
> 4:13 NKJV

The developer of a popular series of business training films describes the phenomenon of discovering your problem-solving skills are going nowhere:

You start thinking, I'm uncomfortable. I'm anxious. I can't do this. I should never have started to try. I'm not creative. I was never creative in school. I'm a complete failure. I'm going to be fired, and that means my spouse will leave me and—in other words, you start enjoying a real, good, old-fashioned panic attack.[4]

Problems can feel ten times larger in the middle of the night. But in reality—and by daylight—solutions might not be as distant as they seem.

Inventor Charles Kettering had a unique problem-solving method. He would divide each problem into the smallest possible pieces, then research the pieces to determine which ones had already been solved. He often found that what looked like a huge problem was already 98 percent solved by others. Then he tackled what was left.

In bite-sized pieces, problems become more manageable. Remember that with God, all things are possible. He can give us peace in our darkest nights and bring wisdom with the morning.

OBSTACLES IN THE PATHWAY OF THE
WEAK BECOME STEPPING-STONES IN
THE PATHWAY OF THE STRONG.

THOMAS CARLYLE

SAY THAT AGAIN?

In 1954, Sylvia Wright wrote a column for the *Atlantic* in which she coined the term "mondegreen," her code word for misheard lyrics. She recounted from her own experience hearing the Scottish folk song, "The Bonny Earl of Morray."

Ye highlands, and ye lowlands,

Oh! whair hae ye been?

They hae slaine the Earl of Murray,

And layd him on the green.

She misheard the last line as "and Lady Mondegreen." It saddened her immensely that both the Earl and the Lady had died. Of course, she was later chagrined to learn that those were not the lyrics at all. But they made so much sense at the time.

Since then, mondegreen collectors have been on the lookout for newer and more comical misunderstandings. For example:

In "America the Beautiful," one young patriot heard, "Oh beautiful, for spacious skies." as "Oh beautiful, for spaceship guys."

Another considered "Away in a Manger" a little unsettling as he sang, "the cattle are blowing the baby away."

Then there was the Mickey Mouse Club fan who, when the cast sang "Forever hold your banners high." thought they were encouraging her to "Forever hold your Pampers high!"[5]

It's no wonder that, with all our earthly static and clamor, we sometimes think we're singing the right words when we're not. But if we begin each day in quiet conversation with God, His Word comes through loud and clear. There can be no misunderstanding God's lyrics.

EARTH CHANGES, BUT THY SOUL
AND GOD STAND SURE.

ROBERT BROWNING

Night Driving

THY WORD IS A LAMP UNTO MY FEET,
AND LIGHT UNTO MY PATH.

PSALM 119:105 KJV

A woman confessed to a friend her confusion and hesitancy about an important life decision she was facing. She professed to believe in God but could not bring herself to rely on her faith to help choose her path.

"How can I know I'm doing the right thing?" she asked. "How can I possibly believe my decision will be right when I can't even see tomorrow?"

Her friend thought and finally said, "Here's how I look at it. You know when you're driving down a dark country road with no streetlights to give you any notion of where you are? It's a little scary. But you rely on the headlights. Now, those headlights may only show you ten yards of road in front of you, but you see where to go for that little stretch. And as you travel that ten-yard stretch of road, the headlights show you ten more yards, and ten more, until eventually you reach your destination safe and sound.

"That's how I feel about living by faith. I may not be able to see tomorrow, next week, or next year, but I know that God will give me the light to find my way when I need it."

WHEN YOU COME TO THE
EDGE OF ALL THE LIGHT
YOU KNOW AND ARE ABOUT
TO STEP OFF INTO THE
DARKNESS OF THE
UNKNOWN, FAITH IS
KNOWING ONE OF TWO
THINGS WILL HAPPEN:
THERE WILL BE SOMETHING
SOLID TO STAND ON, OR
YOU WILL BE TAUGHT
HOW TO FLY.

BARBARA J. WINTER

A Change
of Direction

Two couples on vacation rented a car to drive on the backroads of beautiful British Columbia. Jim and Fran sat in the front; and Fran's mother, Billie, and her stepdad, Dobber, sat in the back.

Jim was driving along when they saw a dirt road angling to the right with the correct highway number posted. Fran said, "Surely that isn't the main road. Maybe the sign was turned. Look, the road straight ahead is paved and lined with utility poles too."

After a lighthearted discussion, the couples took a vote and decided to stay on what appeared to be the main highway. After a few miles, Jim drove up a little hill, and then suddenly all they could see was water, a few small buildings, and a campground sign. The road came to a dead end at a lovely lake and campsite. The couples began laughing as Jim wheeled the car around and headed back to the dirt-road

> THE SHEPHERDS WENT BACK, GLORIFYING AND PRAISING GOD FOR ALL THAT THEY HAD HEARD AND SEEN, JUST AS HAD BEEN TOLD THEM.
>
> LUKE 2:20 NASB

turn they had passed. Eventually, the humble highway meandered into the most magnificent scenery of all.

We can easily stay on the broad, paved road and mindlessly travel to the dead end. Or we can change our thinking and our plans, turn down the narrow road to the Cross, and worship the King. Which will you choose?

THE CROSSROADS ARE DOWN HERE:
WHICH WAY TO PULL THE REIN?
THE LEFT BRINGS YOU BUT LOSS,
THE RIGHT NOTHING BUT GAIN.

ANGELUS SILESIUS

MORNING THIRST

The need for a refreshing drink when we first wake in the morning is often so strong that we find ourselves anticipating the taste before we ever get a glass in our hands. That thirst is a driving force that nothing else will satisfy.

There is another thirst that needs to be quenched when we first wake up. It is a thirst we often ignore until it is so great, that everything else in our lives—relationships, our growth as children of God, our joy, our peace—begins to wither.

Patti did not have running water inside her home when she was a child. Not since then has she known that same level of satisfaction that a morning drink of water can give. This was especially true if the water in the house ran out during the night when it was too cold or too stormy for anyone to make a trip to the source outside. Sometimes it was a long, long wait for morning.

MY SOUL THIRSTS FOR GOD, FOR THE LIVING GOD.

PSALM 42:2 NASB

There is a source of living water that is available to us any time of the day or night. It never runs out, it never gets contaminated, it never freezes over, and it is always as refreshing throughout the day as it was with the first sip in the morning.

Renowned missionary Hudson Taylor said, "There is a living God, He has spoken in the Bible and He means what He says and He will do all that He has promised." He has promised to quench our thirst in such a way that we will never be thirsty again!

Are you anticipating a drink from God's cup of refreshing living water in the morning? God gives you permission to start sipping right now. *Bon appétit!*

EVERY CHARACTER HAS AN INWARD
SPRING; LET CHRIST BE THAT SPRING.
EVERY ACTION HAS A KEYNOTE; LET
CHRIST BE THAT NOTE TO WHICH
YOUR WHOLE LIFE IS ATTUNED.

HENRY DRUMMOND

A WORK IN PROGRESS

> WE ARE HIS WORKMANSHIP, CREATED
> IN CHRIST JESUS FOR GOOD WORKS,
> WHICH GOD PREPARED BEFOREHAND
> THAT WE SHOULD WALK IN THEM.
>
> EPHESIANS 2:10 NKJV

Many centuries ago, a young Greek artist named Timanthes studied under a respected tutor. After several years of effort, Timanthes painted an exquisite work of art. Unfortunately, he was so taken with his painting that he spent days gazing at it.

One morning, he arrived to find his work blotted out with paint. His teacher admitted destroying the painting, saying, "I did it for your own good. That painting was retarding your progress. Start again and see if you can do better." Timanthes took his teacher's advice and produced *Sacrifice of Iphigenia,* now regarded as one of the finest paintings of antiquity.[6]

Timanthes' teacher knew what many great artists know—we should never consider ourselves truly finished with our work.

When the legendary Pablo Casals reached his ninety-fifth year, a reporter asked, "Mr. Casals, you are ninety-five and the greatest cellist who ever lived. Why do you still practice six hours a day?" And Casals answered, "Because I think I'm making progress."

Maya Angelou applies that same logic to daily life. In her book, *Wouldn't Take Nothin' for My Journey Now,* she writes: "Many things continue to amaze me, even well into the sixth decade of my life. I'm startled or taken aback when people walk up to me and tell me they are Christians. My first response is the question 'Already?' It seems to me a lifelong endeavor to try to live the life of a Christian. . . . "[7]

How exciting it is to be a work in progress. With God's help, our possibilities are limitless!

WHAT GOD DOES,
HE DOES WELL.

JEAN DE LA FONTAINE

SUNRISE

Sunrise, shining its beams through the window on a cold winter's morning, is a welcome sight. Even if the air outside is icy cold, sunrise gives the illusion of warmth. With the rising sun, the city opens its shutters and makes preparations for the day; in the country, the farm animals are let out to pasture. Kids are off to school, adults are on their way to work, and each has a different perspective of the sunrise.

THE SUNRISE FROM ON HIGH WILL VISIT US . . . TO GUIDE OUR FEET INTO THE WAY OF PEACE.

LUKE 1:78-79 NASB

Sunrise happens whether we see it or not. Clouds may cover the sky so totally that we can't experience the beauty of the sunbeams making their way to the earth. No matter what the climate, the sun still rises in the eastern horizon and sets over the west. Sunrise is set by God's clock, and it is ours to enjoy in the early mornings when we can see it clearly. It is just as much there for us to enjoy when the clouds cover it. We can trust it to be there—even though it may be hidden for a while.

We can also trust God to be there every morning because He is the one, irrefutable reality in this life, and He remains constant and true!

LIFE IS A MIXTURE OF SUNSHINE AND RAIN, LAUGHTER AND TEARDROPS, PLEASURE AND PAIN—LOW TIDES AND HIGH TIDES, MOUNTAINS AND PLAINS, TRIUMPHS, DEFEATS AND LOSSES AND GAINS. BUT THERE NEVER WAS A CLOUD THAT THE SON DIDN'T SHINE THROUGH AND THERE'S NOTHING THAT'S IMPOSSIBLE FOR JESUS CHRIST TO DO!

HELEN STEINER RICE

MORNING DRIVE

Judy could take the freeway to work each morning and arrive instantly, nerves revved, almost before she is awake. But freeways are ugly. Instead she takes the scenic route around several local lakes and starts her day with mental pictures of sunrises, flowers, and people in various states of running and walking.

Affluence and architecture notwithstanding, she feels that nature is the attraction—a chance for a city slicker to enjoy a little tranquillity. The slower pace gives her the occasion to see a small troop of deer or watch the ducks and geese depart for the winter and return for their spring nesting activities. She recognizes and studies the walkers and joggers who are out regularly at the crack of dawn.

THIS IS THE DAY THE LORD HAS MADE; WE WILL REJOICE AND BE GLAD IN IT.

PSALM 118:24 NKJV

"I don't know if I have a better workday because I sneak up on the job rather than race to it," she muses. "On some mornings, I don't see one thing that nature has to offer because the day ahead refuses to wait for me to get there, and I spend the entire ride making lists of things to do in my head. But I do know that when I take the time to glance at the roses along the way, I feel more fortified, just like our mothers wanted us to be with a hearty breakfast, mittens, and hats."[8]

Taking a few moments to thank God for the glories of creation will make any day start on a better note!

NATURE IS THE ART OF GOD ETERNAL.

DANTE ALIGHIERI

TIME FOR A CHANGE

FAITH IS THE ASSURANCE OF THINGS
HOPED FOR, THE CONVICTION
OF THINGS NOT SEEN.

HEBREWS 11:1 NASB

Skier Jean-Claude Killy was ready to do whatever it took—no matter how hard the work—to be the best when he made the French national team in the early 1960s. But after months of grueling practice, he recognized that his competitors were putting in just as much effort in the same kind of training. It was then he decided to go a step further and find different ways to ski faster rather than just working harder.

He started testing every part of his racing technique, such as altering the accepted leg positions and using his poles in unorthodox ways. Soon, his experiments resulted in an explosive new style that cut his racing times dramatically. Within a few years, Killy won virtually every major skiing trophy and three gold medals in the 1968 Winter Olympics.[9]

Killy learned an important lesson in creativity: Innovations don't require genius—just a willingness to question the norms and try something different.

It's been said that one reason people eventually stop growing and learning is they become less willing to risk failure by trying new ideas or experiences. Change can be difficult and uncomfortable. But if our ambitions are only to avoid the discomforts of life, we could soon find we have very little life at all.

God wants us to have the most joyful, fulfilling life possible, and sometimes that requires stepping out into the unknown. Is there a new experience or idea you've been hesitant to pursue? You'll never know until you try.

IN CREATING, THE ONLY
HARD THING'S TO BEGIN; A
GRASS-BLADE'S NO EASIER
TO MAKE THAN AN OAK.

JAMES RUSSELL LOWELL

BRAVEHEART

Kevin tells the story of a dear friend and fellow church member who passed away after a long life of love and service.

At the funeral, his children stood up one by one to tell stories about their father, and soon a recurring theme became obvious: this man's single most outstanding trait was his willingness to serve others, no matter what the need. He was one of those people who was always ready to lend a hand—to run an errand, do odd jobs, or give someone a ride home. One of his daughters mentioned how everywhere he went, he kept a toolbox and a pair of coveralls in the trunk of his car, "just in case somebody needed something fixed."

> BELOVED, THOU DOEST A FAITHFUL WORK IN WHATSOEVER THOU DOEST TOWARD THEM THAT ARE BRETHREN AND STRANGERS WITHAL.
>
> 3 JOHN 1:5 ASV

More often than not, when we hear the word "courage," we think of heroic acts in times of crisis. But in our everyday lives, we shouldn't overlook the courageousness of simply *being there*. Lives are changed when we faithfully provide for our families, care for the elderly, or lend an ear to a troubled student. Persistence in making this world a better place to live—for ourselves and others—is definitely a form of courage.

Albert Schweitzer, the great Christian missionary, doctor, and theologian, was once asked in an interview to name the greatest living person. He immediately replied, "The greatest person in the world is some unknown individual who at this very moment has gone in love to help another."

AS YOU GO ABOUT YOUR WORK
TODAY, REMEMBER THAT YOU
COULD BE SOMEONE ELSE'S HERO.
HAVE THY TOOLS READY;
GOD WILL FIND THEE WORK.

CHARLES KINGSLEY

THE VALUE OF DISASTER

For ten years Thomas Edison attempted to invent a storage battery. His efforts greatly strained his finances, then in December 1914, nearly brought him to ruin when a spontaneous combustion broke out in his film room. Within minutes all the packing compounds, celluloid for records and film, and other flammable goods were ablaze. Though fire departments came from eight surrounding towns, the intense heat and low water pressure made attempts to douse the flames futile. Everything was destroyed.

While the damage exceeded $2 million the concrete buildings, thought to be fireproof, were insured for barely a tenth of that amount. The inventor's 24-year-old son Charles searched frantically for his father, afraid that his spirit would be broken. Charles finally found him, calmly watching the fire, his face glowing in the reflection, white hair blowing in the wind.

"My heart ached for him," said Charles. "He was 67—no longer a young man—and everything was going up in flames.

When he saw me, he shouted, "Charles, where's your mother?" When I told him I didn't know, he said, "Find her. Bring her here. She will never see anything like this as long as she lives."

The next morning, Edison looked at the ruins and said, "There is great value in disaster. All our mistakes are burned up. Thank God we can start anew." Three weeks after the fire, Edison managed to deliver the first phonograph.[10]

With each new day, we have the opportunity to start again, to start fresh—no matter what our circumstances. Let the Lord show you how to salvage hope from debris. You never know what joys are ahead.

DIFFICULTIES ARE MEANT TO ROUSE, NOT DISCOURAGE. THE HUMAN SPIRIT IS TO GROW STRONG BY CONFLICT.

WILLIAM ELLERY CHANNING

FAITH IS A VERB

In *You Can't Afford the Luxury of a Negative Thought,* John Roger and Peter McWilliams offered a new description of faith. They chose the word *faithing* to describe their proactive approach to confidence in life's outcomes.

In their thinking, faithing works in the present, acknowledging that there is a purpose to everything and that life is unfolding exactly as it should. It is actively trusting that God can handle our troubles and needs better than we can. All we must do is let them go so that He can do His work.

THE TWO BOXES

I have in my hands two boxes
Which God gave me to hold
He said, "Put all your sorrows in the black,
And all your joys in the gold."
I heeded His words, and in the two boxes
Both my joys and sorrows I store,

But though the gold became heavier each day
The black was as light as before.
With curiosity, I opened the black.
I wanted to find out why
And I saw, in the base of the box, a hole
Which my sorrows had fallen out by.
I showed the hole to God, and mused aloud,
"I wonder where all my sorrows could be."
He smiled a gentle smile at me.
"My child, they're all here, with Me."
I asked, "God, why give me the boxes,
Why the gold, and the black with the hole?"
"My child, the gold is to count your blessings,
the black is for you to let go." [11]

FAITH CAN PUT
A CANDLE IN THE
DARKEST NIGHT.

MARGARET SANGSTER

SEEING WITH THE HEART

Maria was a kindhearted teacher's aide who simply wanted to "love the children better" in this class for emotionally disturbed students. She could tolerate much, but Danny was wearing out her patience. It had been easier to love him before, when he would try to hurt himself rather than others. And, although Danny was only seven years old, it really hurt when he would hit her.

GIVE YOUR SERVANT A DISCERNING HEART.

1 KINGS 3:9

For many months Danny would withdraw into a private world and try to hit his head against a wall anytime he got upset. But now, he was making "progress," because instead of withdrawing, he was striking out at Maria.

"Progress?" exclaimed Maria. "How is it progress for him to want to hurt me?"

"Danny was repeatedly abused as a small child," explained the school psychologist. "He has known only adults who were mean to him or simply ignored his most basic needs. He has had no one he could trust. No one to hold him close; no one to dry his tears when he cries or fix him food when he is hungry. He has been punished for no reason. He's making progress, because for the first time in his life, he trusts an adult enough to act out his anger rather than self-destruct. You are that trustworthy adult, Maria."

Upon hearing this explanation, Maria, with tears spilling from her eyes, exclaimed, "I see!" As comprehension dawned, her anger quickly melted.

John Ruskin wrote, "When love and skill work together, expect a masterpiece."[12] Sometimes progress seems elusive, but God is faithful to continue the good work He has started in each of our lives. If we will open the eyes of our hearts, we will see His hand at work in our midst.

IF THERE IS NO STRUGGLE,
THERE IS NO PROGRESS.

FREDERICK AUGUSTUS WASHINGTON BAILEY DOUGLASS

PERFECT HARMONY

The late Leonard Bernstein—conductor, composer, teacher, and advocate—may well be the most important figure in American music of the twentieth century. With his personality and passion for his favorite subject, he inspired generations of new musicians and taught thousands that music should be an integral part of everyone's life.

As a public figure, Bernstein was larger than life—his charm and persuasiveness infectious. While his career progressed, he was constantly sought after for performances, lectures, and other appearances.

But it's said that in his later years, one way his personal life eroded was in his friendships. There came a time when he had few close friends. After his death, a comment from one of his longest acquaintances was that "you wanted to be his friend, but so many other people sought his attention that, eventually, the friendliest thing you could do was leave him alone."[13]

A MAN WHO HAS FRIENDS MUST HIMSELF BE FRIENDLY, BUT THERE IS A FRIEND WHO STICKS CLOSER THAN A BROTHER.

PROVERBS 18:24 NKJV

Scientific evidence now shows us how important friendships are, not only to our emotional health, but physical and mental health as well. But these most cherished relationships are a two-way street. A few tips for keeping friendships on track are:

Be aware of your friends' likes and dislikes. Remember your friends' birthdays and anniversaries. Take interest in your friends' children. Become need sensitive. Keep in touch by phone. Express what you like about your relationship with another person. Serve your friends in thoughtful, unexpected ways.[14]

Good friends are gifts from God. Is there someone you need to call today?

A FRIEND IS ONE WHO
KNOWS ALL ABOUT YOU AND
LIKES YOU JUST THE SAME.

ELBERT GREEN HUBBARD

DR. SIMPSON
AND DANCING

HE HATH PUT IN HIS HEART

THAT HE MAY TEACH.

EXODUS 35:34 KJV

Lively music filled the air as the college students mingled with one another, shared laughs, and danced together. Just then, Dr. Simpson walked up to Rob and asked him, "Why aren't you out there dancing with everyone else?"

"I don't want anyone to laugh at me," he responded.

"What makes you think that they would be looking at you anyway?" came her quick retort with more than a hint of laughter in her voice. She was like that—quick to challenge her students' assumptions, but in a way that provoked thought and self-examination rather than pain and embarrassment.

A respected and admired professor of English, Dr. Simpson expected much from every student. She was tough, but her classes were always full. It was exchanges like this one that made it possible for Rob to see his life from a perspective other than his own, and in gaining this insight he became more self-confident and less uptight. She helped—no, she *forced* him to grow as both a student and a person. Dr. Simpson epitomized the role of teacher.

In the words of one author, "The teacher must be able to discern when to push and when to comfort, when to chastise and when to praise, when to challenge and when to hold back, when to encourage risk and when to protect."[15] This, Dr. Simpson did on a daily basis. And, this is just the type of teacher we need. God usually provides each of us with our own unique Dr. Simpson—many times with more than one.

Are you the kind of teacher who challenges your students to become more than they were before?

A TEACHER AFFECTS
ETERNITY: HE CAN
NEVER TELL WHERE HIS
INFLUENCE STOPS.

HENRY GARDINER ADAMS

GENTLE RIPPLES

Early in the morning, a lake is usually very still; no animals, no people, no noise, no boats, no cars. All is quiet.

This is the best time to skip rocks. By taking a small, flat pebble and throwing it at the right angle, you can skip it across the water, leaving circles of ripples every time it makes contact with the lake. The ripples form small and very defined circles at first, then they spread out and break apart until they vanish. If several people skip rocks at the same time, the ripples cross over one another and blend together to make miniwaves across the lake. The impact can be pretty amazing.

O, GOD, THOU ART MY GOD; EARLY WILL I SEEK THEE.

PSALM 63:1 KJV

For most of us, mornings are filled with so many things that need our attention that we find it difficult to spend time alone with God. However, the Lord set a marvelous example for us by rising early to listen to God. If we make no time for this quiet morning time with God, we often find there is also no time during the day. Then we end up going to bed with regret or guilt. *Maybe tomorrow,* we think. But many times, tomorrow never comes.

When we spend time alone with God at the beginning of each day, we become acquainted with Him and start becoming like Him. Throughout our days, the ripple effect of our time with God in the early morning will have an impact upon the lives of those with whom we have contact.

When these ripples blend with others who spend time with God, we create miniwaves of love and joy. It all starts with a quiet time and a gentle ripple.

A BIT OF THE BOOK IN THE MORNING, TO ORDER MY ONWARD WAY. A BIT OF THE BOOK IN THE EVENING, TO HALLOW THE END OF THE DAY.

MARGARET SANGSTER

SAVED BY THE WEEDS

Farming, like other high-risk occupations, requires a great deal of faith, dependence, and trust in God's timing and goodness.

One year a potato farmer encountered some problems due to hot weather. Because potatoes are a very temperamental crop and must be in the ground a certain period of time, the farmer was concerned that the planting be done on time.

The weather broke, however, and he planted the potatoes only five days late. As the cultivation process began, everything looked good except for two plots where weeds began to grow out of control two weeks before the harvest. It was too late to destroy the weeds. The farmer had to let them keep growing.

"LET BOTH GROW TOGETHER UNTIL THE HARVEST."

MATTHEW 13:30

Another more severe problem emerged when a truck strike interfered with the targeted harvest date. The farmer knew that leaving his potatoes too long in the Arizona summer heat would destroy the crop. In the meantime, the "carpet weeds" continued to flourish and provided an almost blanket-like protection over the potatoes, while taller weeds gave additional shade.

Later as the harvesters examined the fields, they discovered that wherever the weeds had grown up, there was no spoilage of potatoes. In weed-free areas, the potatoes were ruined because of the heat. The weeds saved his crops. He had only 5 percent spoilage.

God often uses seemingly adverse circumstances to shield and shade us from "spoilage" in our lives. The very "weeds" we chafe about—petty irritations, chronic interruptions, "irregular" people—are often the means He uses to enhance our ultimate growth and develop a harvest of Godly character in us.

NOTHING WITH GOD
CAN BE ACCIDENTAL.

HENRY WADSWORTH LONGFELLOW

NEVER GIVE UP

LET US NOT BECOME WEARY
IN DOING GOOD, FOR AT THE
PROPER TIME WE WILL REAP A
HARVEST IF WE DO NOT GIVE UP.

GALATIANS 6:9

Again, the young teacher read the note attached to the fresh green ivy.

"Because of the seeds you planted, we will one day grow into beautiful plants like this one. We appreciate all you've done for us. Thank you for investing time in our lives."

A smile brightened the teacher's face as grateful tears trickled down her cheeks. Like the one leper who expressed gratitude to Jesus for healing him, the students she had taught remembered to say thanks to their teacher. The ivy plant represented a gift of love.

For months the teacher faithfully watered the growing plant. Each time she looked at it, she remembered those special teenagers and was encouraged to continue teaching.

But after a year, something happened. The leaves began to turn yellow and drop—all but one. She started to discard the ivy but decided to keep watering and fertilizing it. One day as she walked through the kitchen, the teacher noticed a new shoot on the plant. A few days later, another leaf appeared, and then another. Within a few months, the ivy was well on its way to becoming a healthy plant again.

Henry Drummond says, "Do not think that nothing is happening because you do not see yourself grow, or hear the whir of the machinery. All great things grow noiselessly."

Few joys exceed the blessings of faithfully investing time and love into the lives of others. Never, never give up on those plants!

GOD DOES NOT PAY
WEEKLY, BUT HE PAYS
AT THE END.

DUTCH PROVERB

BELIEVE IN ME

Cynthia was amazed and grateful for what she was seeing. Ms. Nelson, a fifth grade teacher at the private school where Cynthia worked, was quietly greeting each of the children and their parents at the door of her classroom. Ms. Nelson spoke with pride to each parent of the work of his or her child. She took time to mention the child by name and to point out something about that child's work that was particularly noteworthy. As a result, both the parents and the children glowed with satisfaction.

This was not a special event—it was the morning of a normal school day, and Ms. Nelson made it a habit to be at the door every morning.

As Cynthia stepped into her own office, she was struck by the impact of Ms. Nelson's genuine comments and actions. Cynthia couldn't help but think of a gardener fussing over the flowers and plants of the garden—eager to provide the right nourishment and attention so that each plant grows strong and healthy.

THE LORD MAKE YOU TO INCREASE AND ABOUND IN LOVE ONE TOWARD ANOTHER, AND TOWARD ALL MEN.

1 THESSALONIANS 3:12 KJV

Later that afternoon, Cynthia asked her fifth-grade son John how he liked being in Ms. Nelson's class. John responded, "I like it a lot. She is a really neat teacher because you always know that she believes in you. Even when you don't get everything right, she still believes in you."

What a gift—the ability to believe in others and communicate it to them daily, just as our Lord loves and believes in us without fail. We can all learn to pass this gift on to those we care about.

CORRECTION DOES MUCH, BUT
ENCOURAGEMENT DOES MORE.
ENCOURAGEMENT AFTER CENSURE
IS AS THE SUN AFTER A SHOWER.

JOHANN WOLFGANG VON GOETHE

FOR THE LEAST OF THESE

In Henry Van Dyke's classic, *The Other Wise Man,* Artaban plans to join his three friends in Babylon as they followed the star in search of the King. He has three jewels to offer as gifts to the Christ Child.

But before he arrives, Artaban finds a feverish, poor Hebrew exile in the road. Torn between duty and desire, he ultimately stays and ministers for hours to the dying man. By the time Artaban arrives at the Bethlehem stable, the other Magi have left. A note encourages him to follow them through the desert.

NO ONE HAS EVER SEEN GOD; BUT IF WE LOVE ONE ANOTHER, GOD LIVES IN US AND HIS LOVE IS MADE COMPLETE IN US.

1 JOHN 4:12

But Artaban has given the dying man his last provisions, so he returns to the city, sells one of his three jewels, and buys camels and food. In the deserted town of Bethlehem, a frightened woman cradling her baby tells Artaban that Joseph, Mary, and the Babe fled to Egypt to escape Herod's soldiers who are killing all the baby boys in the city. He offers a ruby to one of Herod's soldiers to save the woman's child.

Heartbroken that he has spent two of his gifts already, Artaban wanders for years, seeking to worship the new King. He discovers no Baby King but finds many poor, sick, and hungry to feed, clothe, and comfort.

Many years later in Jerusalem, white-haired Artaban hears about a king being executed. He rushes toward Calvary to ransom the king with his last jewel. But instead, Artaban ends up rescuing a young woman from slavery.

At the end of the story, Artaban laments the turn of events. He had wanted to bring gifts and minister to the King of kings. Yet he spent his fortune helping people in need. The Lord comforts him with these words: "Verily I say unto you, inasmuch as ye have done it unto one of the least of these my breathren, ye have done it unto me" (Matthew 25:40 KJV).

The celebration of Christmas is more than just a holiday. And worship is more than mere words or gifts. Like the fourth wise man learned, real worship is a way of life.

HE PRAYETH BEST, WHO LOVETH BEST
ALL THINGS BOTH GREAT AND SMALL;
FOR THE DEAR GOD WHO LOVETH US,
HE MADE AND LOVETH ALL.

SAMUEL TAYLOR COLERIDGE

Easy as A, B, C

IN THE DAY OF TROUBLE HE WILL
KEEP ME SAFE IN HIS DWELLING;
HE WILL HIDE ME IN THE SHELTER
OF HIS TABERNACLE AND SET ME
HIGH UPON A ROCK.

PSALM 27:5

"We need to run some tests." Those are words you never want to hear from a doctor. Inundated as we are with medical bulletins, our first inclination is to expect the worst.

Especially intimidating are the machines used to diagnose our disorders. The Magnetic Resonance Imager (MRI), with its oh-so-narrow magnetic metal tunnel, can bring out the claustrophobia in all of us.

A test like this causes a real break in our daily routine. (Have you noticed that most of them are scheduled in the morning?) While we might never reach the point where we look forward to such "breaks," we can do what one woman did to use the time constructively.

Once inside the tube, she found herself on the verge of panic. Then she remembered some advice her pastor had given her: When things are going badly for you, pray for someone else.

To simplify things, she decided to pray alphabetically. Several friends whose names began with *A* immediately came to mind. She prayed for Albert's sore knee, Amy's decision about work, and Andrew's upcoming final exams. She moved on to *B* and continued through the alphabet. By the letter *D,* she was totally oblivious to her environment.

Thirty minutes later, she was only halfway through the alphabet and the test was done. A day later, she used a short "break" in her doctor's office to complete her prayers while she waited for the test results, which showed no abnormalities.

When you find yourself taking a break from your routine that would not be your chosen activity, turn it over to your Father God and watch Him transform it into a special time for the two of you.

HE WHO NEGLECTS
THE PRESENT MOMENT
THROWS AWAY ALL HE HAS.

JOHANN FRIEDRICH VON SCHILLER

GOD KNOWS!

Do you ever wonder if God has lost your address? Perhaps He has lost track of you or even forgotten you? God's Word answers that thought with a resounding, "Not so!"

Jesus taught His followers, "Are not two little sparrows sold for a penny? And yet not one of them will fall to the ground without your Father's leave [consent] and notice. . . . Fear not, then; you are of more value than many sparrows" (Matthew 10:29-31 AMP).

> EVEN THE VERY HAIRS OF YOUR HEAD ARE ALL NUMBERED.
>
> MATTHEW 10:30 AMP

The psalmist also recognized God's thorough and intimate knowledge of us. Read these words from Psalm 139 and be encouraged.

O Lord, you have examined my heart and know everything about me. You know when I sit or stand. When far away you know my every thought. You chart the path ahead of me, and tell me where to stop and rest. Every moment, you know where I am. You know what I am going to say before I even say it. You both precede and follow me, and place your hand of blessing on my head.

This is too glorious, too wonderful . . . I can never be lost to your Spirit! I can never get away from my God! . . .

You saw me before I was born and scheduled each day of my life before I began to breathe. Every day was recorded in your Book!

How precious it is, Lord, to realize that you are thinking about me constantly! I can't even count how many times a day your thoughts turn towards me. And when I waken in the morning, you are still thinking of me!

Psalm 139:1-7, 16-18 TLB

CONSIDER THEN THYSELF, O NOBLE SOUL, AND THE NOBILITY WITHIN THEE, FOR THOU ART HONORED ABOVE ALL CREATURES IN THAT THOU ART AN IMAGE OF GOD; . . . THOU ART DESTINED TO GREATNESS!

MEISTER ECKHART

THE QUIET TOUCH
OF STILLNESS

A late-night snowfall blanketed the city one Saturday. When everyone awoke on Sunday morning, evergreens were layered with sparkling white icing. The roofs of houses looked as if someone had draped each one with a fluffy quilt. Lawns, sidewalks, and streets all blended into an unbroken sea of whiteness.

But more striking than the beautiful whitewash was the pervasive stillness. The city noises were gone. No horns honking or dogs barking. No traffic noise or boom boxes blaring. No doors slamming or machines running. Just stillness—quietness. It almost took your breath away.

IN REPENTANCE AND REST IS YOUR SALVATION, IN QUIETNESS AND TRUST IS YOUR STRENGTH.

ISAIAH 30:15

The quiet didn't last long, however. Soon city snowplows were out, clearing and salting the streets. The sounds of shovels and snowblowers mixed with window scrapers and revving car engines as neighbors began to dig out from the storm. It was not the first snowstorm of the season, nor would it be the last.

But amazingly, that touch of stillness in the morning put everyone in a better mood. Even the coffee tasted better—richer, warmer. Despite the hard work of clearing the heavy snowfall, neighbors called out greetings to each other across the yards, accompanied by groans and laughter and squeals of delight.

The quiet start to the morning left its imprint on the entire day. The pace slowed for a moment, granting people an opportunity for reflection, allowing neighbors time to connect with others. And when normal activities resumed, some people were even able to hold on to the stillness for a while.

When Monday came, it brought with it all the noise of a busy week. But it also brought the remembrance of God's words to His people—that in quietness and trust they would find strength. Let God's quietness fill a corner of your heart today, and find the joy that can be found in stillness. It's a blessing far better than a snowball fight!

ALL THE TROUBLES OF LIFE COME
UPON US BECAUSE WE REFUSE
TO SIT QUIETLY FOR A WHILE
EACH DAY IN OUR ROOM.

BLAISE PASCAL

GUILTY SNACKING

"WATCH AND PRAY SO THAT YOU WILL
NOT FALL INTO TEMPTATION. THE SPIRIT
IS WILLING, BUT THE BODY IS WEAK."

MARK 14:38

Stacie was sitting in the teacher's lounge when she first heard the commotion.

"No way!"

"Check it out!"

"Who's got some quarters?"

Stacie got up and walked cautiously toward the sound of money and elation. She rounded the corner to discover three other teachers gathered around the vending machine. They were inserting change, picking out items, and receiving both the snack and their money back. The machine had a loose wire and was giving out free food.

Stacie grinned. No breakfast that morning and quarters in her pocket made for a happy young woman. She pushed her way through the crowd and gave it a try. Three quarters—some powdered donuts. Three quarters back—a big cinnamon roll. Three quarters back—a bag of chips.

Carrying her quarters and her unexpected breakfast, she headed back to the lounge with a smile on her face.

It wasn't until she sat down that the guilt (and the calories) settled heavily on her conscience. It wasn't right! No matter that everyone else seemed to be OK with it. This was wrong. It was stealing, and she just couldn't do it.

Oh, but how her stomach growled! Surely it would be OK if she had one bite—just one.

Stacie ate it all. But when the vendor came later, she dug into her pocket and paid for all three items. Her co-workers looked at her oddly, but she felt much better.

Today, take a stand for the little acts of truth, the small steps of honesty and courage. Though some may mock you, you just may earn the respect of others, and God will use that to draw them to His heart.

'TIS ONE THING
TO BE TEMPTED,
ANOTHER THING TO FALL.

WILLIAM SHAKESPEARE

A SABBATH

What is it that gives you that warm fuzzy feeling inside? Certain smells, like the aroma of homemade bread right out of the oven or the cinnamony smell of hot apple cider, make you feel everything will be all right.

How about a crackling fire in the fireplace to chase away the damp chill on a rainy night? It makes you feel that life is good.

BE GLAD AND
REJOICE FOR
EVER IN THAT
WHICH I CREATE.

Isaiah 65:18 RSV

What about the whistling of a teakettle ready to brew a pot of your favorite tea? Or listening to a favorite recording of Beethoven's "Moonlight Sonata"? When was the last time you sat outside to do nothing else but watch the sun set?

To Oscar Hammerstein, that warm, fuzzy, everything-is-going-to-be-OK feeling came from "whiskers on kittens and warm, woolen mittens." What are some of *your* favorite things?

When was the last time you gave yourself permission to be nonproductive and enjoy some of life's simple pleasures?

Logan Pearsall Smith wrote, "If you are losing your leisure, look out! You may be losing your soul."

When we don't take time for leisure or relaxation, when we give our discretionary time away to busyness and relentless activity, we are living in a way that says, "Everything depends upon me and my efforts."

Consequently, God prescribed a day of rest, the Sabbath, to enjoy His creation, to give us time to reflect and remember all He has done for us and all that He is. The Sabbath is time to remember God is God—and we're not!

The Sabbath doesn't have to be Sunday. You can take a Sabbath rest anytime you relax and turn your focus to God and His creation. Sometimes you have nothing better to do than relax. You may have something *else* to do, but you don't have anything *better* to do.

Relax and just enjoy God's creation. After all, He created it for you to enjoy.

THERE IS NO MUSIC IN A REST, BUT THERE IS THE MAKING OF MUSIC IN IT.

JOHN RUSKIN

THE CONTEST

It was a typical day in first grade, and while their teacher was tending to other students, Sammy and Molly were engrossed in a discussion of the utmost importance: Who was taller?

Molly was one of the smaller children in the class, but that never interfered with her keen sense of competition. When Sammy declared his superior height, she responded by sitting up tall and straight.

When Sammy sat up taller and straighter, Molly stood up beside her desk.

When Sammy stood up across the aisle and immediately overshadowed her, Molly—after stealing a glance across the room to ensure her teacher's back was still turned—stepped up on her chair.

When the teacher finally turned to check on the commotion, the two children were standing atop their desks, on their tiptoes, stretching for all they were worth!

Children are typically excited about getting bigger, and the wise adult still seeks growth. Those who lose this zest die long before their funerals.

How long has it been since you felt the thrill of growing—of improving some aspect of your life? You may have felt it as you graduated from high school, received your first promotion on the job, learned a new craft, or ran in your first 5K race. The desire for growth is a powerful incentive in our lives.

If improving in size, career, or talent is exciting, other aspects of our lives can bring even more lasting satisfaction. Growing in our relationship with God is one of them. In fact, taking our desires for growth to the Lord can result in a double blessing—gaining His strength and vision for improving our lives, while deepening our joy in knowing Him.

BE NOT AFRAID OF GROWING SLOWLY,
BE AFRAID ONLY OF STANDING STILL.

CHINESE PROVERB

LIFE LESSONS

SPEAKING THE TRUTH IN LOVE.

EPHESIANS 4:15 KJV

"You know that what you did was wrong, don't you?"

The words echoed in Sandra's mind as she went home from school that evening. She was a good student who had never cheated in her life. Yet, this last assignment had been more than she could handle. In a moment of desperation, she copied the work of another student.

Her teacher, Mrs. Wallace, had asked her to wait after class, and Sandra knew what was coming. Still, it was a shock when Mrs. Wallace asked her if it was really her work.

"Yes," she squeaked out, then wondered why she had lied.

Looking her straight in the eye, Mrs. Wallace carefully said, "You know that what you did was wrong, don't you? Take tonight to think about your answer, and I will ask you again in the morning if this is your work."

It was a long night for Sandra. She was a junior in high school with a well-deserved reputation for honesty and kindness. She had never cheated before, and now she had compounded her mistake by deliberately lying—and to someone she admired and loved. The next morning she was at Mrs. Wallace's classroom door long before school officially started, and she quietly confessed her misdeed. She received the appropriate consequences, a zero on the assignment and detention (her first and only detention).

Years later, Sandra often thought of that experience and felt gratitude for loving correction from someone she respected. Mrs. Wallace was willing to help Sandra make honest choices—even on the heels of making a dishonest one. For Sandra, this was a life lesson about taking responsibility for past mistakes and choosing honesty no matter what the consequences.

TO BE HONEST AS THIS
WORLD GOES, IS TO BE
ONE MAN PICKED OUT
OF A THOUSAND.

WILLIAM SHAKESPEARE

FLOWERBOX FAITH

One Labor Day weekend, Shannon's husband constructed a large flowerbox for her. With great care, she picked out and purchased two hundred top-quality bulbs. Next, she filled the flowerbox with the perfect mixture of soil, fertilizer, and peat moss. Then, she spent hours planting the bulbs in a delightful design.

ON MY BED I REMEMBER YOU; I THINK OF YOU THROUGH THE WATCHES OF THE NIGHT. BECAUSE YOU ARE MY HELP, I SING IN THE SHADOW OF YOUR WINGS. MY SOUL CLINGS TO YOU; YOUR RIGHT HAND UPHOLDS ME.

PSALM 63:6-8

All through the long Idaho winter, she thought about her tulips, daffodils, and hyacinths. If they followed God's plan and waited for His perfect timing, they would change from dull, brown clumps into colorful celebrations of spring.

Maintaining our faith in God during times of forced inactivity is similar to a dormant bulb planted in a flowerbox. At certain times in our lives, we may be compelled to stop all activity and take time out to heal. Instead of lying in our beds fretting about our restraining circumstances, we simply need to wait and rest.

Dormancy for a bulb is nature's solution to getting through times of difficult weather conditions. God's gift of rest is His way of helping us through difficult health conditions. All bulbs store food to carry them through their dormant periods. We can use our times of dormancy to nourish our souls by planting our hearts in the fertile soil of His Scriptures.

Like bulbs waiting for spring, we can rest in God's promises as we wait for our recovery. We can look forward to the certain celebration of life through Christ. He alone will bring the colors of spring to our souls.

FAITH IS NOT BELIEVING THAT
GOD CAN, BUT THAT GOD WILL!

ABRAHAM LINCOLN

STRESS AND SERENITY

"**H**on,**" the petite supermarket employee said in her southern drawl, "everybody I know says they are *just worn out.*" She took a deep breath, brushed a wisp of unruly brunette hair away from her blue eyes, and continued checking groceries.

Stress has become a buzzword for Americans, especially in the last decade. At some point in our lives, we are all overcome with hectic schedules and perfectionistic tendencies.

In his article, "Confessions of a Workaholic," psychiatrist Paul Meier wrote, "Having grown up with an overdose of the Protestant work ethic, I was an honor student who was somewhat overzealous . . . I was a first-class workaholic and I was proud of myself for being one. I thought that was what God wanted of me."[16]

But later through the help of friends, the conviction of the Holy Spirit, and biblical teaching, Dr. Meier established new priorities. At the top of his list was: "Know God personally."

AFTER HE HAD SENT THE CROWDS AWAY, HE WENT UP ON THE MOUNTAIN BY HIMSELF TO PRAY; AND WHEN IT WAS EVENING, HE WAS THERE ALONE.

MATTHEW 14:23 NASB

He observed, "I've learned to accept living in an imperfect world. Every need is not a call for my involvement. I have learned to trust God instead of myself to rescue the world. He can do a much better job of it anyway."

Jesus, too, must have been exhausted by demands placed upon Him. When He departed to pray in quiet solitude, He left a significant example for us to follow—daily.

Ask the Father to help you make quietness a priority so that, regardless of the time of day, you can go to the garden alone and hear His voice.

DO NOT LOOK FORWARD TO WHAT MAY HAPPEN TOMORROW; THE SAME EVERLASTING FATHER; WHO CARES FOR YOU TODAY, WILL TAKE CARE OF YOU TOMORROW, AND EVERY DAY. EITHER HE WILL SHIELD YOU FROM SUFFERING OR HE WILL GIVE YOU UNFAILING STRENGTH TO BEAR IT.

SAINT FRANCIS OF SALES

TESTED BY FIRE

HE HAS SAID TO ME, "MY GRACE
IS SUFFICIENT FOR YOU, FOR
POWER IS PERFECTED IN WEAKNESS."

2 CORINTHIANS 12:9 NASB

Many gardens are outlined by evergreen trees—some large and some small. The lodgepole pine is a tall, stately tree found in the high Western mountains. Commonly seen in Yellowstone National Park, the hardwood is also valuable for making railroad ties and poles. Its fragrant needle-shaped leaves grow in bundles and produce fruit—a woody pine cone, which takes two years to mature.

An interesting feature of the lodgepole is its response to fire. When flames attack the tree, the heat causes the cones to burst. The seeds are then dispersed, and natural reforestation occurs. New growth begins, and a fresh forest eventually replaces the charred remains.

During life's trials, the fruit of our lives is also tested. Our spiritual maturity is revealed by how we respond. Do we see God's hand at work, even when our hearts are scorched by pain and sorrow? Have we become intimately acquainted with our Savior so that we know He will somehow use it for good?

When a young child was near death, friends gathered at the hospital to pray with the parents. Another mother, grieving over the loss of her own son, watched the praying group. Although the other child also died, the mother later received Christ as a result of the family's testimony. Both mothers shared a tremendous loss; but they also share a bright hope of one day seeing their boys again in Heaven.

After enduring the fires of adversity, we often learn that others have been watching. Through trusting Him, their barren souls will burst into life and yield fruit for His glory.

GRACE DOES NOT
DESTROY NATURE,
IT PERFECTS IT.

SAINT THOMAS AQUINAS

HOLY LAUGHTER

The air was filled with peals of laughter along with giggles of delight and chortles of joy. Just hearing it made Ron's day better. His mother had run a licensed day-care facility in their home for as long as he could remember, and dozens of children from single-parent households benefited from her unconditional love. In fact, it was easy to think of their home as an oasis of love in a world lacking in it.

> HE WILL YET FILL YOUR MOUTH WITH LAUGHTER AND YOUR LIPS WITH SHOUTS OF JOY.
>
> JOB 8:21

Ron remembered the December morning when four-year-old Louis came in from the cold and quite seriously said, "It's winter out there Reen (short for Irene)!" as he struggled to pull his arms free from his heavy coat.

Or the time when Jeffrey came by to visit and hand deliver an invitation to his high school graduation. "Grandma Reen" had cared for him throughout his elementary school years. Ron remembered Jeffrey coming from school each day of third grade. He and his best friend would exit the school with their arms draped around one another's shoulders and walk that way all the way to the bus.

Many, many other memories existed. But the best, without a doubt, was that of the joyous laughter of the children as they played together. There was something so natural and carefree about the sound that anyone who heard it would know that this place was a world of safety and love—thanks to "Grandma Reen."

Have you had the chance to listen to the laughter of small children lately? Take time to listen, and your soul will be refreshed.

LAUGHTER IS THE MUSIC OF LIFE.

SIR WILLIAM OSLER

FIELD OF DREAMS

There was nothing special about Randy. Each year his teachers repeated the same words: "You don't want Randy in your class. He's a loser."

But that was before he entered Miss Jewel's sixth grade art class. Until then, only bright red Ds and Fs adorned Randy's school papers. Test scores plummeted him to the bottom 10 percent of his class.

Miss Jewel saw the sparkle in Randy's eyes when he watched her demonstrations. His huge, rough fingers took to a paintbrush like an athlete to sports. Charcoals, sculpting, watercolor, oils—whatever the project, Randy excelled beyond any student Miss Jewel had ever seen.

HOPE DEFERRED MAKES THE HEART SICK, BUT A LONGING FULFILLED IS A TREE OF LIFE.

PROVERBS 13:12

She challenged him to take private lessons and suggested the names of several artists she knew. Randy made excuses for not pursuing the lessons, but Miss Jewel suspected it was because of his family's poverty.

The teacher decided to make Randy her special project. Year after year she saved her money. On Randy's graduation from high school, she sent him an anonymous check to cover his college tuition—and the name of an artist who agreed to teach Randy in the summers between his college studies.

One day about ten years later, she received a package in the mail—a beautiful oil painting of herself. And these words: "I will never forget you. I have dedicated my life to helping others grow their dreams like you did for me. Thank you. Randy."

God may give each of us a "Randy" to nurture— perhaps a child, a friend, a student, or coworker. Our words, our time, even our belief in their ability could help produce a crop of doctors, musicians, presidents, or simply loving moms or dads who will rise in their own "field of dreams."

YOU CANNOT TEACH A MAN
ANYTHING; YOU CAN ONLY
HELP HIM TO FIND IT HIMSELF.

GALILEO GALILEI

Rise and Shine

"TAKE MY YOKE UPON YOU AND
LEARN FROM ME, FOR I AM GENTLE
AND HUMBLE IN HEART, AND YOU
WILL FIND REST FOR YOUR SOULS."

MATTHEW 11:29

Janie jolted awake at the sound of her alarm clock. This was her third day waking up in the middle of the night—at least it felt like the middle of the night, even though it was actually early morning. She was not at all sure why she was going to the trouble. It especially seemed vague and worthless the moments before her head settled back down onto the pillow.

"No!" She yelled at herself, waking up again with a start. She had promised she would do this, and she was going to, even if she went around for the rest of the day with a sleep-deprived, grumpy attitude. Janie stumbled to the bathroom, splashed some water on her face, and carefully traversed the steps. Downstairs, she started a pot of coffee and sat down at the kitchen table. She had originally started doing her devotions on the sofa, only to discover they only lasted the five minutes it took for her to fall asleep again. At the kitchen table, she took out her Bible, her notebook, and a devotional. Her attitude brightened.

Once she was up, every moment was worth it. Meeting God in the early morning hours didn't make her grumpy as she always anticipated, but instead it revitalized her and brought her peace. It took awhile to convince her body of the benefits of such early rising, but soon it became habit. After a while, the only time she experienced grumpiness was when she missed her morning meeting with God.

God's yoke *is* light; He *is* the rest for our souls that we think sleep should bring. Taking the time with our Savior in the early morning hours is better than fine cappuccino or the smell of omelets and bacon. It is the best part of our day.

WHEN JESUS IS PRESENT,
ALL IS GOOD AND
NOTHING SEEMS DIFFICULT;
BUT WHEN JESUS IS
ABSENT, ALL IS HARD.

THOMAS Á. KEMPIS

SACRIFICE AT SEA

Captain Eddie Rickenbacker, a famous World War I pilot, was forced down into the Pacific Ocean while on an inspection trip in 1942. The plane, a B-17, stayed afloat just long enough for all aboard to get out. Amazingly, Rickenbacker and his crew survived on rubber rafts for almost a month.

"I AM THE LIVING BREAD THAT CAME DOWN FROM HEAVEN. IF ANYONE EATS OF THIS BREAD, HE WILL LIVE FOREVER. THIS BREAD IS MY FLESH, WHICH I WILL GIVE FOR THE LIFE OF THE WORLD."

JOHN 6:51

The men braved high seas, unpredictable weather, and the broiling sun. Night after night, they fought sleep as giant sharks rammed the rafts. But of all their enemies at sea, one was by far the worst—starvation.

After eight days at sea, all of their rations were gone or ruined by the salt water. They knew that in order to survive, they needed a miracle. According to Captain Eddie, his B-17 pilot conducted a worship service and the crew ended it with a prayer for deliverance and a hymn of praise. Afterwards, in the oppressive heat, Rickenbacker pulled down his hat and went to sleep.

"Something landed on my head," said Rickenbacker. "I knew that it was a seagull. I don't know how I knew, I just knew." He caught the gull, which was uncharacteristically hundreds of miles from land. The gull, which seemed to offer itself as a sacrifice for the starving men, was something Captain Eddie never forgot.

In the winter of his years, every Friday evening at about sunset, Captain Eddie would fill a bucket with shrimp and feed the seagulls along the eastern Florida coast. The slightly bowed old man with the gnarled hands would feed the gulls, who seemed to come from nowhere. He would linger awhile on the broken pier, remembering a time when a seagull saved his life.

Jesus offered Himself as a sacrifice too. He is the Living Bread that came from Heaven. And just as Captain Eddie never forgot what one seagull meant to him, let's never forget what Christ did for us. Share the Bread of Life with those who are hungry.[17]

REST OF THE WEARY, JOY OF THE SAD, HOPE OF THE DREARY, LIGHT OF THE GLAD, HOME OF THE STRANGER, STRENGTH TO THE END, REFUGE FROM DANGER, SAVIOR AND FRIEND!

JOHN SAMUEL BEWLEY MONSELL

SONLIGHT IN
MY GARDEN

Martha badgered Johnny all year to plant her a garden. Finally, he agreed. Together they tilled the soil, preparing it with the best additives, including peat moss, landscape mix, soil conditioners, and bark mulch.

Martha disliked the flowers in her local nursery, so she begged Johnny to let her order some unique varieties out of a mail-order catalog. Gingerly, she selected each one, often choosing the most expensive plants. *It will be the prettiest yard in the neighborhood,* she thought. *No one can match these beauties.*

GROW IN THE GRACE AND KNOWLEDGE OF OUR LORD AND SAVIOR JESUS CHRIST.

2 PETER 3:18

The tender plants arrived in the mail, and Martha began working immediately. She planted and watered; she fertilized; she watched; and she waited. But nothing happened. One by one, the leaves turned yellow and began to wilt. By the end of spring, not one plant remained. They all shriveled and died.

Martha wrote a scathing letter to the mail-order nursery demanding her money back.

Two weeks later, she received a reply.

"Madam, your letter indicated you planted your flowers in a beautiful shady area and fed them the best nutrients possible. Your flowers failed to grow for the following reason: You planted them in the wrong place. You ordered flowers that must face the sun. Although you took great care to prepare the soil, without exception, these particular plants will die without sunlight. Next time, please read the directions before ordering your flowers and planting your garden."

Our lives are like that. We may spend great amounts of care and dollars to make ourselves beautiful. But if we are not facing the Son, we will wilt and eventually die. No amount of expensive "additives" will take the place of adequate Sonlight in our souls.

FROM MORNING TO NIGHT KEEP JESUS
IN YOUR HEART, LONG FOR NOTHING,
DESIRE NOTHING, HOPE FOR NOTHING,
BUT TO HAVE ALL THAT IS WITHIN YOU
CHANGED INTO THE SPIRIT AND
TEMPER OF THE HOLY JESUS.

WILLIAM LAW

SEND IN THE CLOWNS

When the circus came to town, posters went up on the grocery store bulletin boards, billboards announced the performance dates, and television commercials urged listeners to "Come one; come all!" Lion tamers, wire walkers, and trapeze artists were part of the three-ring extravaganza. But the most anticipated performers were the clowns. With their crazy antics and outlandish costumes, they livened up each performance.

Clowns work hard at their profession. In fact, in order to travel with the Ringling Brothers Circus, clowns must successfully complete clown college—an intense course of study that covers everything from makeup to pratfalls, costuming to making balloon animals, juggling to sleight of hand. Only after clowns have mastered all of these skills can they take their place in the circus ring.

As Sheila stood at the stove sautéing vegetables for supper, she sensed a connection to this group of performers in the circus. Though she didn't wear a clown costume or clown makeup, she worked hard at juggling—balancing her time among home, family, students, friends, and church. She wasn't skilled at card tricks or sleight of hand, but she could work "magic," explaining math concepts in ways any student could understand. And while she might not know the ins and outs of balloon-animal art, Sheila made lots of other things, from costumes for school plays to crafty Christmas gifts and decorated birthday cakes.

God's Word says that we are to work at whatever we do with all our hearts, remembering that whatever we do is for the Lord. Whether we're clowns or cooks, tightrope walkers or teachers, we need to work hard at our professions. And when we do, we might just provide our students and families with some laughter along the way!

THE AVERAGE PERSON
PUTS ONLY 25 PERCENT OF
HIS ENERGY AND ABILITY
INTO HIS WORK.

ANDREW CARNEGIE

THE GOD OF TOMORROW

When the microwave buzzed, Rebecca slid her chair away from her laptop computer and retrieved the hot water for her tea. She had been writing an article about new technologies and how they would impact our lives in the next century. The whole topic was unsettling. The more research she did on the Internet, the more disturbed she became about cloning, supercomputers, and spy satellites. Where would it all end?

I AM THE LORD—
I DO NOT
CHANGE.

MALACHI 3:6 TLB

Suddenly, she had an urge to hear the comforting whistle of a teakettle and the crackling of a real fire instead of the hiss of a gas log. The world was moving too fast, and at times like these, she wanted to crawl up in her grandpa's lap and smell his sweet cherry pipe.

"Grandpa," she remembered asking one time, "did you have spaceships when you were little?"

He chuckled. "No, honey, when I was a little boy, we rode in a horse-drawn wagon to town. Airplanes had just really gotten off the ground."

"But you had trains."

"Yep, I guess I always liked trains the best."

The sound of a train whistle still reminded her of Grandpa and how he looked in his navy-blue conductor's uniform. Sometimes he would let her dress up in it and carry around his big silver watch. "All aboard!" she'd call, and Grandpa would pretend to be a passenger.

I wonder what Grandpa would think about life today? She knew. He'd tell her not to worry. "Honey," he'd say, "I've been in some pretty tight places in my day: train wrecks, labor strikes, and world wars. I reckon if God pulled us through all of that, He can see us the rest of the way home."

She "reckoned" He would. The God of her grandpa's era would be the same God today. And that's a comforting thought.

GOD IS AND THAT NOT IN TIME
BUT IN ETERNITY, MOTIONLESS,
TIMELESS, CHANGELESS ETERNITY,
THAT HAS NO BEFORE OR AFTER;
AND BEING ONE, HE FILLS ETERNITY
WITH ONE NOW AND SO REALLY IS.

PLUTARCH

CHANGING SEASONS

Marie had always enjoyed washing dishes by hand. It gave her an opportunity to slow down, think, and observe the changing of the seasons as she gazed out her kitchen window.

Over the course of a year, Marie watched a sparrow preparing her nest and then bringing food to her babies in the springtime. A hummingbird made regular stops after he discovered the window feeder during the summer. In autumn, squirrels scampered around in the crisp fallen leaves in search of acorns. During the winter, Marie saw a deer standing majestically in her yard.

THE GRASS WITHERS AND THE FLOWERS FALL, BUT THE WORD OF OUR GOD STANDS FOREVER.

ISAIAH 40:8

As the cycle of seasons began again, Marie watched flowers pop up through the soil when the weather got warmer. Their brilliantly colored blossoms always brought her happiness. In the summer, the green grass filled her heart with peace and tranquility. And as the green leaves gradually transformed to shades of gold, she sensed the autumn nip in the air, a sure sign that winter would follow.

Life is like the changing seasons. During the springtime of Marie's life, her days were filled with fun and joy as she played with frogs and tadpoles. Her teen and young adult years—the summer of her life—were marked by enthusiasm as she tried to find herself in the fast lane of life. Today, Marie is beginning to sense the contentment of autumn. She sees security in the eyes of her husband and joy in the lives of her grown children and realizes that winter soon will be upon her.

As a Christian, Marie knows that one day she will awaken to a world more wonderful than she can even imagine. Until then, she knows that whatever season she's in right now is the best season of her entire life.

There's nothing wrong with looking back at the previous seasons of our lives. But God has a purpose for allowing us to be in the season we're in right now. So enjoy where you are on the way to where you're going!

LIFE CAN ONLY BE UNDERSTOOD
BACKWARDS; BUT IT MUST
BE LIVED FORWARDS.

SØREN AABYE KIERKEGAARD

THE BETTER WAY

SINCE, THEN, YOU HAVE BEEN RAISED
WITH CHRIST, SET YOUR HEARTS ON
THINGS ABOVE, WHERE CHRIST IS
SEATED AT THE RIGHT HAND OF GOD.

COLOSSIANS 3:1

Martha was a dedicated homemaker. She was an expert at entertaining her guests while preparing a scrumptious meal at the same time. One day when Jesus was passing through the village, Martha opened her home to Him. Her house was spotless, and the aroma coming from her kitchen was delightful. As a wonderful hostess, she made sure that Jesus felt welcome in her home.

Her sister, Mary, also was there. While Martha opened her home to Jesus, Mary opened her heart to Him and sat at His feet. She knew that true wisdom would be hers if she listened to His teachings and applied them to her everyday life.

Meanwhile, Martha began to grumble. She felt that Mary should be more involved in the work at hand. She went to Jesus to ask Him to send her sister to help her in the kitchen.

Jesus' response probably surprised her. He taught Martha some things about priorities, while sharing with her a better way to serve Him. Mary, He said, had chosen the better way, and it would not be taken away from her.

What are the priorities in your life? Do you take time out of your busy schedule to read God's letter to the world?

While working and serving are vital parts of living, they cannot be the most important part. Seek God's guidance today through prayer and Bible study. The wisdom that you gain will benefit not only you but others as well, as your life serves as a shining example for Him.

AS IN PARADISE, GOD
WALKS IN THE HOLY
SCRIPTURES, SEEKING MAN.

SAINT AMBROSE

SOMEONE WHO CARES

Maureen wearily rinsed out her coffee cup and stacked it in the nearly full dishwasher. Her life had been difficult for months. As her husband's illness rapidly progressed, her sense of security waned, and a fear of losing him filled her heart. After a few weeks in the hospital, her husband of forty-five years was forced to live in a nursing home. It seemed that Maureen couldn't stop crying. Her heart felt heavier after each visit.

At first, people asked if there was anything they could do to help. Others telephoned and visited her. But after a few weeks, the calls and visits dwindled as her friends got on with their lives. She was overcome with weariness, and joy seemed so remote.

One day before she left for her daily visit to the nursing home, she stopped by the mailbox. A small "thinking of you" card was tucked inside. It was signed, "Someone who cares." A ray of sunshine touched her heart as she read those simple words.

Someone really cares, she thought. She didn't know who it was, but she knew that someone was concerned about the situation that overshadowed her life. All day long she wondered who had been so kind. She looked at the card over and over, trying to see if she could recognize the signature. She knew that the person was praying for her, and she wanted to let her know how much she appreciated it.

As the weeks and months passed, Maureen continued to receive greeting cards from this anonymous person. The signature was always the same. But no one ever confessed to being the sender. Only God knew who uplifted her spirit. And for the sender, that was enough.

WHAT BRINGS JOY TO THE HEART IS
NOT SO MUCH THE FRIEND'S
GIFT AS THE FRIEND'S LOVE.

SAINT AILRED OF RIEVAULX

HIDE AND SEEK

When Lucille's children were young, they enjoyed playing hide-and-seek in the dark. The old country kitchen with its cavernous cupboards and deep recesses contained many good places to hide. On one such occasion, one of their cousins—the smallest one, in fact—curled up in the back of the cupboard where Lucille kept her baking pans. When the pans were moved close to the cupboard door, the child was virtually invisible behind them. It was an ideal hiding place.

With a shout of "Ready or not, here I come!" the game started. One by one, the hiding places and hidden children were found. But the littlest cousin, curled up in the baking-pan cupboard, evaded discovery. An older child would have been thrilled at not being found. But this child didn't see things that way. Sipping a cup of tea in the darkened kitchen, Lucille heard a tiny voice whimper, "Isn't anyone going to come looking for me?" That little voice was all it took for the rest of the children to locate their cousin. Though the others congratulated him on his hiding place, he was just glad someone had found him.

Though Paul wasn't playing hide-and-seek, the Bible tells us that he had been hidden in Tarsus

BARNABAS WENT TO TARSUS TO LOOK FOR SAUL.

ACTS 11:25

for quite some time. He could have easily felt abandoned by the other believers. He could have wondered if anyone even cared to know where he was. But then God sent Barnabas to find Paul. And when Barnabas found him, the two of them began a missionary journey that would ultimately change their world for Christ.

Though we may not play hide-and-seek anymore as grown-ups, we can sometimes feel buried under responsibilities and schedules that close in on us and hide us from time with friends and family. That's when we need someone like Barnabas—someone to seek us out and show us that they care.

Do you know someone who needs a Barnabas? Reach out—with a note, a phone call, a prayer, or a visit—and do a little seeking, not hiding, today.

A CHARGE TO KEEP I HAVE,
A GOD TO GLORIFY;
A NEVER-DYING SOUL TO SAVE,
AND FIT IT FOR THE SKY.

CHARLES WESLEY

Wrong Route

WAIT FOR THE LORD; BE STRONG AND
TAKE HEART AND WAIT FOR THE LORD.

PSALM 27:14

Downtown Seattle, sitting in the hotel lobby and waiting for a bus—Lizzy and Karen had broken free of a conference and were ready to explore the city that surrounded them. They'd been waiting for the bus for twenty minutes and found themselves impatient and eager. There was so much to do—so much to see!

Moments later, a bus pulled up. "It's not the one they said we should take," Lizzy said, smiling as she began walking toward the doors, "but it's headed in the same direction! Let's go!" They climbed on board—two Midwestern girls, heading for the sights. As the bus made its way through the dark and scary underbelly of the city, the girls huddled together in a small corner of the bus. The driver seemed amused by their predicament, and their fellow passengers seemed anything but willing to help them find their desired destination. They grasped each other's hands and tried to look less like tourists and more like residents. That only served to emphasize their discomfort.

Lizzy and Karen ended up staying on the bus for the whole route. Arriving back at the hotel, they were slightly shaken but had only lost a little time. They grinned at each other ruefully and waited—and waited—and waited for the right bus.

Is there a bus you're tempted to climb aboard because you're tired of waiting? Is there a relationship, a job, a direction you're thinking of taking that may not be God's best for you? There is much to be gained by waiting in the lobby for the right bus. God will not abandon you in your search. He is there, ready and waiting with His answer, reminding you of His sovereign will and His ability to take you where you need to go. It's OK to wait on Him. In fact, it's much safer and a whole lot wiser, especially when you consider the alternative.

ALL COMES AT THE
PROPER TIME TO HIM WHO
KNOWS HOW TO WAIT.

SAINT VINCENT DE PAUL

NOWHERE TO HIDE

"**H**ow did you know I was here?" Patty rested her head against the steel post of the bridge and swung her legs gently over the water below.

"Where else would you be?" her husband, David, asked. He stood behind her, respecting her need for space. "This is where you always come when your heart hurts. After three years, you don't think I know that?"

WHERE CAN I GO FROM YOUR SPIRIT? WHERE CAN I FLEE FROM YOUR PRESENCE?

PSALM 139:7

Patty beckoned him to sit beside her. "In a way, I'm glad you know." He sat down. "I come out here to be alone, but I don't really want to be alone. Part of me needed you to know . . . to search and find me. I wanted to know that someone cared enough to worry about how I was doing." She paused. "I guess that's silly, huh?"

David took her hand in his. "No, it's not silly." He said nothing else. He just sat there, quietly supporting and loving her, knowing she needed to be alone but not alone, separate but still loved.

Our Heavenly Father knows us even more intimately than our own spouses do. When we try to run and hide from God's presence, He is always there—not as an intruder or an accusing presence, but as a loving companion. He is a friend who holds us even when we're afraid to look Him in the eye. His love knows no hiding place. There is nothing to run from if we belong to Him. So often He won't speak a word when we try to escape Him. He just waits, acknowledging our choices and loving us just the same.

Have you run away from your Father? He is there if you want to talk to Him. He knows your heart, and He wants to be with you. Even in the moments of aloneness, God is your silent companion.

GOD FAR MORE DWELLS IN ME THAN IF THE ENTIRE SEA WOULD IN A TINY SPONGE WHOLLY CONTAINED BE.

ANGELUS SILESIUS

WHAT'S WRONG, HONEY?

Phyllis will never forget the day God answered one of her prayers in a miraculous way. Pregnant and at home with her two children, Phyllis had no means of transportation. Her husband, Carl, worked on the road and was driving their only car. She had no idea where he was, and as much as they wanted one, they could not afford a cellular phone.

The morning was going well for Phyllis. Her five-year-old twins played in their room while she cleaned house. Around lunchtime, she heard a loud thump. Just as she got to their bedroom door, she saw one twin sail off the top bunk. They had been warned not to play up there, but their desire to fly was just too great. The first twin had landed safely, but the second broke his arm, learning the hard way that little boys can't fly.

Carl wouldn't be home for several hours, and since she couldn't reach him, she immediately called her father to take her and the children to the hospital. She cradled her screaming son while waiting for her dad. Wanting Carl to know

"EVERYONE WHO ASKS RECEIVES; HE WHO SEEKS FINDS; AND TO HIM WHO KNOCKS, THE DOOR WILL BE OPENED."

MATTHEW 7:8

the situation, she cried out to God to have Carl call home. Just as she said, "Amen," the phone rang.

"What's wrong, honey?" Carl asked. For several seconds, she was speechless.

"How did you know something was wrong?" she asked.

"I just had a feeling," he said. After she told him the news, her father arrived. Carl met them at the hospital.

Phyllis was thankful that her line of communication to God was open and that He immediately relayed the message to Carl, saving them both a lot of fear and worry. That line is always open. But you have to call first! Today, sharpen your communication skills by spending some time in prayer.

IF THE SKY FALLS,
HOLD UP YOUR HANDS.

SPANISH PROVERB

BLOOM WHERE YOU ARE TRANSPLANTED

> YOU WILL BE LIKE A WELL-WATERED
> GARDEN, LIKE A SPRING WHOSE
> WATERS NEVER FAIL.
>
> ISAIAH 58:11

A young couple moved to a new city, far from family and friends. The movers arrived; the couple unpacked their belongings, and the husband started his job the following week. Each day when he arrived home, his wife greeted him at the door with a new complaint.

"It's so hot here."

"The neighbors are unfriendly."

"The house is too small."

"The kids are driving me crazy."

And each afternoon, her husband would hold her gently and listen to her gripes. "I'm sorry," he would say. "What can I do to help?"

His wife would soften and dry her tears, only to begin the same scenario the next afternoon.

One evening her husband walked through the front door with a beautiful flowering plant. He found a choice spot in the backyard and planted it. "Honey," he said, "every time you feel discontented, I want you to go and look at your garden. Picture yourself as that little flowering plant. And watch your garden grow."

Every week he brought home a new tree, flowering shrub, or rose bush and planted them in the backyard. Each morning she watered the garden and measured its progress. Friendships grew with other women on her block, and they asked her for gardening help. Soon, they were seeking spiritual advice as well.

Our Heavenly Father knows that we must all learn to bloom where we are transplanted. With His wise, loving touch, we will not only flourish, but we can produce the ever-blooming fruit of love, kindness, and contentment.

WHEN LIFE ISN'T THE
WAY YOU LIKE IT, LIKE
IT THE WAY IT IS.

JEWISH PROVERB

Playful Joy

Grandma Lu watched her grandson, a bit perplexed by his actions. Benjamin, in all his six-year-old glory, was spinning. Not for any apparent reason, he was simply spinning, around and around and around. His little arms were stretched out on either side of his body, and his head was thrown back as a deep belly laugh escaped from his rosy lips. It didn't seem that he was doing much—hardly anything amusing or interesting.

Grandma Lu paused.

[THERE IS] A
TIME TO WEEP
AND A TIME
TO LAUGH.

ECCLESIASTES 3:4

Was there something fun about spinning? She glanced around the lobby of the hotel where she sat. There were only a few people nearby, and they were buried deep in magazines and newspapers. She stood up and set her purse on the seat, blushing even as she walked toward her spinning grandson. She wasn't sure if there was any special technique, so she watched him for a moment before spreading out her own arms. She began slowly at first, careful not to bump into anything, worried she might slip and fall. Then she threw caution to the wind and began to speed up. She threw her head back and laughed, and felt the momentum of her own body carry her in circles. What fun!

A few minutes later, she slowed to a stop. Benjamin stood before her, his mouth open, his eyes wide. He began to laugh, and she laughed with him. They made quite a pair in that hotel lobby—disheveled, flushed, spinning grandmother and grandson. But people smiled, because their joy was real.

Laughter is God's gift of healing for a saddened heart. It gives lightness to the spirit and gets the blood flowing. Find a way to laugh today; rent a funny movie, read the comics, or play with a child and forget you're an adult. Do things you wouldn't normally think of doing and allow yourself to enjoy it. There is a time to laugh. Take that time today and revel in the abandonment of playful joy.

JOY IS THE MOST INFALLIBLE SIGN
OF THE PRESENCE OF GOD.

LÉON HENRI MARIE BLOY

THE GOD WHO
NEVER SLEEPS

In March of 1975, a tornado raked an eight-mile path across Atlanta, Georgia, snapping pine trees like toothpicks. Civil defense officials estimated the damage to be as high as thirty million dollars.

Even today, Gloria remembers that day as though it were yesterday. She was a younger woman then and had worked part-time as a secretary at a small office. The office was closed that Monday, so employees could attend a memorial service for a coworker.

That morning as Gloria got ready for the service, she noticed the skies outside turn an ominous black. The wind picked up, and trees bowed like rubber. She watched metal garbage cans being tossed down the street. Then the driving rain hit. The last thing on Gloria's mind, though, was a tornado.

After attending the service, she drove home. Visibility was poor as the rain slanted in sheets across the road. When she passed by her office, she almost wished she had gone to work, so she wouldn't have to battle the weather all the

CAST ALL YOUR
ANXIETY ON HIM
BECAUSE HE
CARES FOR YOU.

1 PETER 5:7

way home. The constant scraping of the windshield wipers grated on her nerves, so she turned on the radio to drown out the sound. The news reports were unbelievable! A tornado had been spotted in the Atlanta area. She accelerated, urging her car toward home.

Not until later did she learn that the tornadoes that whipped through Atlanta had destroyed the building where she worked. When she finally went back to the office and surveyed the damage, she found everything in shambles. She trembled when she saw the collapsed concrete wall on top of her desk and shuddered to think what might have happened had she gone to work.

What a blessing to know that God is omnipresent! He is the One who neither slumbers nor sleeps. He promises to be with us and deliver us even in the midst of a whirlwind. Look to God when darkness blankets your world, and He will show you the way home!

THE WISE MAN IN THE STORM PRAYS TO GOD, NOT FOR SAFETY FROM DANGER, BUT FOR DELIVERANCE FROM FEAR. IT IS THE STORM WITHIN THAT ENDANGERS HIM, NOT THE STORM WITHOUT.

RALPH WALDO EMERSON

CLOSING THE DOOR

WE WANT EACH OF YOU TO SHOW THIS
SAME DILIGENCE TO THE VERY END,
IN ORDER TO MAKE YOUR HOPE SURE.

HEBREWS 6:11

Michelle looked around her office and felt a sigh rise from the depths of her soul. She had worked so hard for all of this and had put so many hours into her vision, especially at the beginning, when her company had only been a dream and her energy was committed to making the dream come true. Someone else had appreciated her creativity—a bigger, larger company that had bought her out in a forceful merger. Now all that was once hers belonged to an unseen face. It was like losing a family member.

Michelle looked out of her office window at her employees. She knew they had been looking to her, waiting to see how she would handle herself over the past four weeks. She was tempted to throw all her energy into a new pursuit, but she also knew that she had a commitment to see this old one to its end. It was a matter of integrity. The new company would never know if she spent her time—their time now—on this new pursuit. But she would know, and her employees would know. No, when she finally handed this company over, she would do so knowing that she had done her best to the very end.

Change takes place in all of our lives. One season ends, and another begins. We may say good-bye to a job, a relationship, a town, or a dream. With each ending, we have a choice. We can walk away without looking back, ignoring the closure and attention that's needed, or we can take the time to finish well—to tie up loose ends, to say our good-byes, to work hard right to the end. Only then can we know we have closed out the old chapter with integrity.

Is there an area of your life that needs attention today? Something that needs to be finished well? Take a moment and ask God to help you close the door. Then you can face your new beginning with confidence.

THE CROSSROADS ARE
DOWN HERE: WHICH
WAY TO PULL THE REIN?
THE LEFT BRINGS YOU
BUT LOSS, THE RIGHT
NOTHING BUT GAIN.

ANGELUS SILESIUS

THE STORMS OF LIFE

One cold winter day in the 1960s, a major ice storm hit central Georgia. Power outages were rampant throughout the area. Some people owned fireplaces or gas heaters, but others who were less fortunate were forced to seek shelter in the homes of their neighbors.

One particular family didn't have any source of heat except for the gas stove in their kitchen. For days, while they huddled together around the kitchen table, the heat from the oven kept them warm.

They could cook, while some of their hapless neighbors could not. Many nearby residents brought over cans of soup to heat on their stovetop. Hospitality intensified as a bitter cold spell set in.

Sitting around that table and the glow of a single candle, the family laughed and shared stories and events that were important to each of them. They hadn't done that in months! While the television

WE KNOW THAT IN ALL THINGS GOD WORKS FOR THE GOOD OF THOSE WHO LOVE HIM, WHO HAVE BEEN CALLED ACCORDING TO HIS PURPOSE.

ROMANS 8:28

was out of order, they put their lives back into place. As a result of that storm, the family grew closer. Each one of them remembered the light from that candle for years afterwards.

Sometimes we don't realize what's missing in our lives until we cease all of our busyness. Spending quality family time together is important to God. But you don't need to wait for an ice storm or some other crisis to draw your family close.

God is always faithful to show goodness in every situation. Just as the glow of the candle provided light during the storm, He lights our way through the darkest and most difficult days of our lives.

DIFFICULTIES ARE MEANT TO ROUSE,
NOT DISCOURAGE. THE HUMAN SPIRIT
IS TO GROW STRONG BY CONFLICT.

WILLIAM ELLERY CHANNING

FUTURE FATHER

June surveyed the crowd before her. The noise seemed too much, almost overwhelming as everyone tried to speak at once. It was Sunday dinner, and all the family was gathered around the large table. Steaming platters of food were being handed from person to person as plates were piled higher and higher with delectable treats.

Down near the end of the table sat Daniel, a friend of June's youngest child, Nate. Daniel was only eight years old and looked flustered and nervous as people passed food around and over him. June watched as one of the other children noticed and attended to him. "Would you like some of these potatoes, Daniel?"

"WHOEVER WELCOMES A LITTLE CHILD LIKE THIS IN MY NAME WELCOMES ME."

MATTHEW 18:5

The small boy nodded and smiled a simple grin of appreciation. The others seemed to take notice of him then and began asking him questions about school and friends. June knew that Daniel had a difficult home life. She was proud of her children as they focused on his hopes and dreams and seemed genuinely interested. "What do you want to be when you grow up?" asked one of the children.

Daniel hesitated and looked around at the family. "I want to be a dad. With lots of kids, like this family."

The room got quiet as everyone mulled over what he had said. Finally Bob, the oldest, smiled broadly and patted Daniel on the back. "Sounds great, Daniel! You'll make a great father," he said, winking, "as long as you have a better group than this one to work with!"

The room exploded as all the kids laughed and began shouting over each other, yelling their defense. June watched Daniel in the rising commotion. He was sitting quietly with a smile on his face. Finally he grabbed his fork and seemed to nod to himself as he ate his first big bite. He seemed—triumphant.

Is there a little one you can love on today? Someone in your home, your class, or your neighborhood? Just a few small words of encouragement and a pair of listening ears can make a difference in the life of a child.

THE DEEPEST PRINCIPLE IN
HUMAN NATURE IS THE CRAVING
TO BE APPRECIATED.

WILLIAM JAMES

Eat Your Breakfast!

Breakfast is the most important meal of the day.

This phrase and others like it have become well known in our culture, but it isn't just Mom's advice anymore! Scientists and doctors have spent millions of dollars to discover what moms have known all along.

Even more important than a naturally nutritious breakfast, however, is a spiritually nutritious breakfast. David said in Psalm 63:1 (NKJV): "O God, You are my God; Early will I seek You." Jesus once said to His disciples, "I have food to eat of which you do not know," then He explained: "My food is to do the will of Him who sent Me, and to finish His work" (John 4:32, 34 NKJV).

When we spend the first part of our day in the Word of God, prayer, meditation, and praise and worship, we acquire an inner strength and energy that adds vitality to our entire day. This "food for the soul" is truly food that the world does not know about. Regardless of where our day may take us or the situations we may encounter, we have a renewed mind to think the thoughts of God, to feel His heartbeat, and to say and do what Jesus would say and do.

After having breakfast with God, you will be prepared to face whatever the day may bring—and end the day with less stress and frustration. When you make your relationship with the Lord your top priority, you are setting yourself up for blessings all day!

GOD REVEALS HIMSELF
UNFAILINGLY TO THE
THOUGHTFUL SEEKER.

HONORÉ DE BALZAC

First Cup

Many people wouldn't dream of starting their day without a cup of coffee. They count on that "first cup of the day" to wake them up and get them going.

There are others who have discovered an even more potent day-starter: first-thing-in-the-morning prayer.

For some, this is a prayer voiced to God before getting out of bed. For others, it is a planned time of prayer between getting dressed and leaving for work. For still others, it is a commitment to get to work half an hour early to spend quiet, focused time in prayer before the workday begins.

IN THE MORNING MY PRAYER COMES BEFORE YOU.

PSALM 88:13 NKJV

Henry Ward Beecher, one of the most notable preachers of the nineteenth century, had this to say about starting the day with prayer:

In the morning, prayer is the key that opens to us the treasure of God's mercies and blessings. The first act of the soul in early morning should be a draught at the heavenly fountain. It will sweeten the taste for the day.

. . . And if you tarry long so sweetly at the throne, you will come out of the closet as the high priest of Israel came from the awful ministry at the altar of incense, suffused all over with the heavenly fragrance of that communion."[18]

A popular song in Christian groups several years ago said, "Fill my cup, Lord; I lift it up, Lord. Come and quench this thirsting of my soul. Bread of heaven, feed me till I want no more; Fill my cup, fill it up and make me whole."[19]

Morning prayer is a time to have your cup filled to overflowing with peace. And the good news is—unlimited free refills are readily available any time your cup becomes empty throughout the day!

BETWEEN THE HUMBLE AND
CONTRITE HEART AND THE MAJESTY
OF HEAVEN, THERE ARE NO BARRIERS;
THE ONLY PASSWORD IS PRAYER.

HOSEA BALLOU

SHARE THE SECRET

A woman named Frances once knew a young person at church named Debbie. Debbie always seemed effervescent and happy, although Frances knew she had faced struggles in her life. Her long-awaited marriage had quickly ended in divorce. She had struggled to get a grip on her single life. She hadn't chosen it, but she decided she would live it with utmost enjoyment and satisfaction. Debbie was active in Sunday school, in the choir, as a leader of the junior high girls' group, and in the church renewal movement.

Frances enjoyed knowing Debbie. Debbie's whole face seemed to smile, and she always greeted Frances with a hug. One day she asked Debbie, "How is it that you are always so happy—you have so much energy, and you never seem to get down?"

With her eyes smiling, Debbie said, "I know the secret!"

"What secret is that?" Frances asked.

Debbie replied, "I'll tell you all about it, but you have to promise to share the 'secret' with others."

Frances agreed, "OK, now what is it?"

I HAVE LEARNED THE SECRET OF BEING CONTENT.

PHILIPPIANS 4:12

"The secret is this: I have learned there is little I can do in my life that will make me truly happy. I must depend on God to make me happy and meet my needs. When a need arises in my life, I have to trust God to supply according to His riches. I have learned most of the time I don't need half of what I think I do. He has never let me down. Since I learned that secret—I am happy."

Frances' first thought was, *That's too simple!* But upon reflecting over her own life, she recalled how she thought a bigger house would make her happy—but it didn't! She thought a better-paying job would make her happy—but it hadn't. When did she realize her greatest happiness? Sitting on the floor with her grand-children, eating pizza and watching a movie—a simple gift from God.

Debbie knew the secret, Frances learned the secret, and now you know it too!

'TIS BETTER TO BE LOWLY BORN,
AND RANGE WITH HUMBLE LIVES IN
CONTENT, THAN TO BE PERKED UP
IN A GLISTERING GRIEF, AND
WEAR A GOLDEN SORROW.

WILLIAM SHAKESPEARE

TALK WITH THE CREATOR

WISDOM BEGINS WITH RESPECT FOR
THE LORD; THOSE WHO OBEY HIS
ORDERS HAVE GOOD UNDERSTANDING.

PSALM 111:10 NCV

"There is literally nothing that I have ever wanted to do, that I asked the blessed Creator to help me do, that I have not been able to accomplish. It's all very simple if one knows how to talk with the Creator. It is simply seeking the Lord and finding him." These are the words of the great scientist, George Washington Carver, the American botanist who literally rebuilt the southern agricultural economy after the Civil War.

Born a slave, Carver eventually became head of the Agriculture Department at Tuskegee Institute in Alabama. He developed more than three hundred uses for the peanut and dozens of products from the sweet potato and the soy bean. Much of Carver's research was conducted in his laboratory, which he called "God's Little Workshop."

"No books are ever brought in here," he said, "and what is the need of books? Here I talk to the little peanut, and it reveals its secrets to me. I lean upon the twenty-ninth verse of the first chapter of Genesis. 'And God said, Behold I have given you every herb bearing seed which is upon the face of all the earth, and every tree in the which is the fruit of a tree yielding seed; to you it shall be for meat.'"

Carver had a habit of seeking the Lord early in the morning. He said, "There He gives me my orders for the day. I gather specimens and listen to what God has to say to me. After my morning's talk with God I go into my laboratory and begin to carry out His wishes for the day."[19]

You can begin each day asking your Creator what He would have you do that day and how He would have you do it! If you are facing a challenge, God can reveal a new perspective. If you need inspiration, God can stir you up. If you feel you are in a dead-end situation, God can show you His way out. Seek your Creator today!

WISDOM IS OFTENTIMES
NEAR ER WHEN WE STOOP
THAN WHEN WE SOAR.

WILLIAM WORDSWORTH

STRAIGHT AHEAD

The sun is barely up and that annoying alarm clock is blaring in your ear. Groggily you reach over and fumble around until you hit the snooze button. *Just a few more minutes,* you think, *and then I can get up and face the day.* The alarm sounds again. You know you can't put it off any longer.

After a couple of cups of coffee, your brain is finally humming. Now the question is, which of today's tasks should you tackle first? Before you head off to school, you might seek inspiration from this prayer, written by Jacob Boehme, a German shoemaker who was born more than 400 years ago:

> IT IS GOD WHO ARMS ME WITH STRENGTH AND MAKES MY WAY PERFECT.
>
> 2 SAMUEL 22:33

Rule over me this day, O God, leading me on the path of righteousness. Put your Word in my mind and your Truth in my heart, that this day I neither think nor feel anything except what is good and honest. Protect me from all lies and falsehood, helping me to discern deception wherever I meet it. Let my eyes always look straight ahead on the road you wish me to tread, that I might not be tempted by any distraction. And make my eyes pure, that no false desires may be awakened within me.[20]

A DAY WITHOUT DISTRACTIONS, FOCUSED ONLY ON THE IMPORTANT. A DAY VIEWED THROUGH PURE EYES. A DAY MARKED BY GOODNESS AND HONESTY. A DAY OF CLEAR DIRECTION AND NO DECEPTION. A DAY WITHOUT FALSEHOOD AND LIES. A DAY IN WHICH GOD'S WORD RULES OUR MINDS AND HIS TRUTH REIGNS IN OUR HEARTS. NOW THAT'S A DAY WORTH GETTING UP FOR!

WILLIAM COWPER

GIVE YOUR BEST

Mrs. Gibson's kindergarten class filed onto the stage. This was the day they had all waited and practiced for. The children bounced with excitement, every boy and girl dressed in his or her Christmas best. The stage was a plethora of red, white, green, smiles, and wiggles!

The program progressed smoothly. Mrs. Gibson smiled at the children, and they smiled back. They seemed to remember every instruction she had given them before they went on stage. Mrs. Gibson began to relax and enjoy the presentation.

Chris was one of the last children to speak and stepped proudly to the microphone. He took a deep breath and began. "The Wise Men brought their best gifts to Jesus. They brought Gold, Frankenstein, and Smurfs."

Chris got quite an ovation. He lingered for a moment behind the microphone, chest thrust out, all smiles. He had done his best.

> "FROM EVERYONE WHO HAS BEEN GIVEN MUCH, MUCH WILL BE DEMANDED; AND FROM THE ONE WHO HAS BEEN ENTRUSTED WITH MUCH, MUCH MORE WILL BE ASKED."
>
> LUKE 12:48

That is all any of us can do. God gave His very best gift to us. When we bring our gifts to Jesus, they don't have to be perfect. They just need to be our best, given from a heart of love.

GIVE OF YOUR BEST TO THE MASTER,

NAUGHT ELSE IS WORTHY HIS LOVE;

HE GAVE HIMSELF FOR YOUR RANSOM,

GAVE UP HIS GLORY ABOVE; LAID

DOWN HIS LIFE WITHOUT MURMUR,

YOU FROM SIN'S RUIN SAVE; GIVE

HIM YOUR HEART'S ADORATION,

GIVE HIM THE BEST THAT YOU HAVE.

HOWARD B. GROSE

True Value

In the J. M. Barrie play, *The Admirable Crichton*, the earl of Loam, his family, and several friends are shipwrecked on a desert island. These nobles were adept at chattering senselessly, playing bridge, and scorning poorer people. However, they could not build an outdoor fire, clean fish, or cook food—the very skills they needed to survive.

What the earl's family and friends did know was entirely useless for their survival. Had it not been for their resourceful butler, Crichton, they would have starved to death. He was the only one who possessed the basic skills to sustain life. In a great turnabout, Crichton became the group's chief executive officer.

It is always good to remind ourselves of our "relative" place in society. If we are on top, we need to remember we can soon be at the bottom. If we perceive ourselves as at the bottom, we need to know that in God's order we are among "the first."

In *The Finishing Touch,* Chuck Swindoll raises the issue of perceived significance by asking about the people behind these Christian greats:

> Who taught Martin Luther his theology and inspired his translation of the New Testament?
> Who visited with Dwight L. Moody at a shoe store and spoke to him about Christ?
> Who was the elderly woman who prayed faithfully for Billy Graham for over twenty years?
> Who found the Dead Sea Scrolls?
> Who discipled George Mueller and snatched him from a sinful lifestyle?[21]

We may not achieve the fame and recognition from people that we would like to have in this life, but God doesn't call us to be well known or admired. He calls us to be faithful to Him in whatever situation we find ourselves. When we are, we can see more clearly when he promotes us and gives us favor with others.

HE WHO KNOWS
HIMSELF BEST ESTEEMS
HIMSELF LEAST.

HENRY GEORGE BOHN

On the Road Again

Getting yourself out of bed in the morning is one thing. Feeling prepared to face whatever comes your way that day is another. Where do you turn for a confidence-booster?

Believe it or not, one of the best confidence-builders you can find may be inside those fuzzy slippers you like to wear: your own two feet.

Researchers have discovered that regular exercise—thirty minutes, three or four times a week—boosts the confidence level of both men and women. This is due in part to the way exercise strengthens, tones, and improves the body's appearance. It also has to do with brain chemistry.

When a person exercises, changes take place inside the brain. Endorphins, released as one exercises, are proteins that work in the pleasure centers of the brain and make a person feel more exhilarated. When the heart rate increases during exercise, neurotrophins are also released, causing a person to feel more alert and focused.

> GOD DID NOT GIVE US A SPIRIT OF TIMIDITY, BUT A SPIRIT OF POWER, OF LOVE, AND OF SELF-DISCIPLINE.
>
> 2 TIMOTHY 1:7

Are you feeling anxious about your day? Take a walk, jog, cycle, or do some calisthenics first thing in the morning. See if you don't feel a little more on top of the world.

Those who exercise regularly also feel that if they can discipline themselves to exercise, they can discipline themselves to do just about anything!

The human body is one of the most awesome examples of God's creative power—an example we live with daily. He has created us not only to draw confidence from reading His Word and experiencing His presence through prayer, but also from the use of our body.

Put on those walking shoes and talk with God as you go! Not only will your body become more fit and your mind more alert, but the Holy Spirit will give you direction and peace about your day.

GOD GIVES TO EVERY MAN THE
VIRTUE, TEMPER, UNDERSTANDING,
TASTE THAT LIFTS HIM INTO LIFE
AND LETS HIM FALL JUST IN THE
NICHE HE WAS ORDAINED TO FALL.

WILLIAM COWPER

PERSONAL IDEALS

What do you hold to be your personal ideals—the qualities you consider to be foremost in defining good character?

This is what Sir William Osler once said about his own ideals:

I have three personal ideals. One, to do the day's work well and not to bother about tomorrow. . . . The second ideal has been to act the Golden Rule, as far as in me lay, toward my professional brethren and toward the patients committed to my care. And the third has been to cultivate such a measure of equanimity as would enable me to bear success with humility, the affection of my friends without pride, and to be ready when the day of sorrow and grief come to meet it with the courage befitting a man.

A speech teacher once assigned her students to give a one-sentence speech, entitled "What I Would

Like for My Tombstone to Read." The class told her later that this assignment was one of the most challenging assignments they had ever received. In virtually every case, the students saw a great discrepancy between the way they lived their lives and the way they desired their lives to be perceived by others.

Many of us make New Year's resolutions to "turn over a new leaf." We greet a new day with a vow or determination to "do better" in a certain area of our lives. But rarely do we give diligent thought to what we consider the highest and noblest pursuits in life.

This morning, give some thought to what *you* hold to be the characteristics of a respected life. What do *you* aspire to in your own character?

As you identify these traits, you can then see more clearly how you desire to live your life and what must change in order to live up to your ideals.

FAME IS VAPOR; POPULARITY
AN ACCIDENT, RICHES TAKE WINGS.
ONLY ONE THING ENDURES
AND THAT IS CHARACTER.

HORACE GREELEY

MORE THAN
POSITIVE THINKING

AS HE THINKS IN HIS HEART,
SO IS HE.

PROVERBS 23:7 NKJV ·

What we think about determines what we do. Even more important, the Scriptures tell us that what we think about shapes our attitudes and how we live our lives.

The Greek city of Philippi was one of the places where the apostle Paul had a fruitful ministry. The Greeks were great thinkers. They loved a good debate, a lively conversation about philosophy, or a rousing time of oratory that might trigger the imagination. Paul wrote to the Philippians:

> Whatever things are true, whatever things are noble, whatever things are just, whatever things are pure, whatever things are lovely, whatever things are of good report, if there is any virtue and if there is anything praisewor-thy—meditate on these things.
>
> Philippians 4:8 NKJV

It's interesting to note Paul wrote this immediately after addressing three other concerns in Philippians, chapter 4. First, he told two women who were having an argument to become of "the same mind in the Lord." Paul wanted them to be at peace with each other and to rejoice together in the Lord.

Second, Paul told them to be gentle with all men. That's descriptive of having peace with those who don't know the Lord. And third, Paul advised them not to be anxious or worried about anything, but to turn all their troubles over to the Lord. He wanted them to have total peace of mind and heart.

As we look for the good in others and meditate on the unending goodness of our Creator, we find the path toward peace with others and the peace that passes all understanding in whatever situation we find ourselves.

Thinking right is more than positive thinking—it is living a life that is filled with God's goodness, wisdom, and mercy!

THE SOUL IS TINGED
WITH THE COLOR
AND COMPLEXION OF
ITS THOUGHTS.

MARCUS AURELIUS ANTONINUS

THE BULLDOG WAY

Are you in the midst of a frustrating struggle? Before you throw in the towel, remember this story about the bulldog.

A man once owned two very fine bird dogs, and he had spent many hours training them. One day he looked out his window just in time to see an ugly little bulldog digging his way under the fence into his bird dogs' yard. As the dog wriggled under the fence, the man realized it was too late to stop him.

He thought to himself how uneven the fight would be. The poor little bulldog was surely no match for his animals. Snipping, barking, growling—tails and ears flying—the battle raged. When the little dog had had enough, he trotted back to the hole under the fence and shimmied out.

> LET US NOT BE WEARY IN WELL DOING: FOR IN DUE SEASON WE SHALL REAP, IF WE FAINT NOT.
>
> GALATIANS 6:9 KJV

Amazed that none of the dogs looked any the worse from the fight, he didn't give the incident another thought until the next day, when he saw the little bulldog coming down the sidewalk toward the hole in the fence. To his amazement, a repeat performance of the previous day's battle began. And once again, the little bulldog picked his moment to end the fight, left the bird dogs barking and snarling, and casually slid back under the fence.

Day after day for over a week, the unwelcome visitor returned to harass his bigger canine counterparts. Then the man was obliged to leave for a week on business. When he returned, he asked his wife about the ongoing battle.

"Battle?" she replied, "Why there hasn't been a battle in four days."

"He finally gave up?" asked the bird-dog owner.

"Not exactly," she said. "That ugly little dog still comes around every day. He even shimmied under the fence until a day or so ago. But now all he has to do is *walk* past the hole and those bird dogs tuck their tails and head for their doghouse whining all the way."

SOMETIMES PERSISTENCE IS
THE KEY TO SUCCESS! IF WELL
THOU HAST BEGUN, GO ON
FORERIGHT; IT IS THE END THAT
CROWNS US, NOT THE FIGHT.

ROBERT HERRICK

THE PEOPLE FACTOR

Wanted: Someone willing to risk his life to rescue 200 Jewish artists and intellectuals from the Nazis. Faint of heart need not apply.

Would you jump at the chance to take on this job? Varian Fry did. A high-school Latin teacher from Connecticut, he went to Marseilles, France, in August 1941, intending to stay only three weeks. He stayed fourteen months.

Forging passports and smuggling people over the mountains into Spain, Fry and a handful of American and French volunteers managed to save almost 4,000 people from the Nazi scourge. Among them were the 200 well-recognized Jewish artists and intellectuals he originally intended to rescue.

GREATER LOVE HATH NO MAN THAN THIS, THAT A MAN LAY DOWN HIS LIFE FOR HIS FRIENDS.

JOHN 15:13 KJV

Did Fry have a difficult time motivating himself each day to face the task in front of him? Probably not. He had little doubt that what he was doing had divine purpose and tremendous significance.

Most of us will never find ourselves in Fry's position, and often we wonder if what we do throughout our day has any significance at all. In many cases, it takes more strength to do the trivial tasks than the monumental ones.

If the job we do is difficult, we must ask God to show us how to make the task less strenuous. If the job is dull, we need to ask God to reveal ways to make it more interesting. If we think our work is unimportant, we need to remember that being in God's will and doing a good job for Him will not only bring blessing to others, but will bless to us now and for eternity.

Often it is the *people* factor that keeps us motivated. God gives us purpose and makes our lives meaningful, but He is always working to bless us, so we can turn around and bless other people.

The tasks you face today are significant as you work to meet a need or to see growth in others. You will see God's love moving through your life to others in everything you do for them—from putting a bandage on a child's skinned knee to inventing a machine that helps people with asthma breathe.

ALL SERVICE RANKS
THE SAME WITH GOD.

ROBERT BROWNING

JIGSAW PUZZLE

> LOOKING AWAY [FROM ALL THAT WILL
> DISTRACT] TO JESUS, WHO IS THE LEADER
> AND THE SOURCE OF OUR FAITH [GIVING
> THE FIRST INCENTIVE FOR OUR BELIEF]
> AND IS ALSO ITS FINISHER [BRINGING
> IT TO MATURITY AND PERFECTION].
>
> HEBREWS 12:2 AMP

Are you a jigsaw puzzle afficionado?

If you have ever worked a complicated jigsaw puzzle, you know three things about them:

First, they take time. Few people can put several hundred pieces of a puzzle together rapidly. Most large and complex puzzles take several days, even weeks, to complete. The fun is in the *process*, the satisfaction in the *accomplishment*.

Second, the starting point of a puzzle is usually to identify the corners and edges, the pieces with a straight edge.

Third, jigsaw puzzles are fun to work by oneself but even more fun to work with others. When a "fit" is discovered between two or more pieces, the excitement is felt by all the participants.

Consider the day ahead of you to be like a piece in the jigsaw puzzle of your life. Indeed, its shape is likely to be just as jagged, its colors just as unidentifiable. The meaning of today may *not* be sequential to that of yesterday. What you experience today may actually *fit* with something you experienced several months ago or something you will experience in the future. You aren't likely to see the big picture of your life by observing only one day. Even so, you can trust that there is a plan and purpose. All the pieces will come together according to God's design and timetable.

The main thing to remember is to enjoy the process. Live today to the fullest, knowing one day you'll see the full picture.

FAITH IS THE DARING OF
THE SOUL TO GO FARTHER
THAN IT CAN SEE.

WILLIAM NEWTON CLARKE

LOVE YOUR ENEMIES

With the Cold War over, Americans and Russians seem to be looking at each other in a new way. Imagine being an American soldier stationed in Bosnia-Herzegovina, working alongside your Russian counterparts. How do you work together after decades of mistrust?

HOW GOOD
AND PLEASANT
IT IS WHEN
BROTHERS LIVE
TOGETHER IN
UNITY!

PSALM 133:1

American and Russian officers who were asked this question agreed that when it comes right down to it, people are people, and soldiers are soldiers. When there's a goal to reach, one finds a way to communicate. The mission is kept in focus, ground rules are established, language barriers are overcome, mutual interests are discovered, and before long, friendships develop!

The early Christian believers certainly thought they had an enemy in Saul of Tarsus, and the feeling was mutual. Saul was extremely active in persecuting Christians in Jerusalem and was determined to deal the same harsh blows to believers in Damascus. But then Jesus appeared to him, and his life was dramatically changed.

Believers in Damascus were suspicious of Saul when he arrived and declared he was also a believer in Jesus Christ. But as they witnessed his manner of living, God dramatically changed their hearts. In the end, the apostle *Paul* became an ardent friend of believers everywhere.

Have you secretly been at "war" with a coworker or neighbor? Beginning today make a concerted effort to find common ground with that person. Smile when your instincts tell you to grimace. Stay focused on your goals and stick to the ground rules when working or volunteering together. Talk to him or her. Seek out hobbies, concerns, or family interests you hold in common. Start treating the person as you would a friend, not an enemy. After all, it's when your enemy is no longer your enemy that the fun begins!

MEN WHO WALK IN THE WAYS
OF GOD WOULD NOT GRIEVE THE
HEARTS EVEN OF THEIR ENEMIES.

SA'DI

WHICH LIFESTYLE?

The word *lifestyle* has been popular for several decades. In simplest terms, this word denotes how we live from a financial standpoint, the possessions we choose to buy, and how much money we have to spend.

A great deal is being written these days about the simple life—downshifting or downscaling. At the same time, we see an ongoing exaltation in our culture of all that is excessive. As a nation, we seem to love peering into the lifestyles of the rich and famous. We envy them. Every few minutes television commercials tell us to buy more and better possessions.

The two paths—one toward a materially leaner life and the other toward a materially fatter life—are like opposite lanes on a highway. We are going either in one direction or the other. We are seeking to discard and downsize or to acquire and add.

"GOD SO LOVED THE WORLD, THAT HE GAVE."

JOHN 3:16 NASB

The Scriptures call us to neither a Spartan nor an opulent lifestyle, but rather, to a lifestyle of *generosity*—a life without greed or hoarding. A life of giving freely, a life of putting everything we have at God's disposal. Our lifestyle is not about how much we earn, what we own, or where we travel and reside. It's how we relate to other people and how willing we are to share all we have with them.

In *Visions of a World Hungry,* Thomas G. Pettepiece offers this prayer: "Lord, help me choose a simpler life-style that promotes solidarity with the world's poor . . . affords greater opportunity to work together with my neighbors."

As you touch your various possessions throughout the day—from the appliances in your home to your clothing and your vehicle—ask yourself, "Would I be willing to loan, give, or share this with other people?" Then ask the even tougher question, "Do I actually share, loan, or give of my substance on a regular basis to others?"

HE WHO GIVES WHAT HE WOULD
AS READILY THROW AWAY, GIVES
WITHOUT GENEROSITY; FOR
THE ESSENCE OF GENEROSITY
IS IN SELF-SACRIFICE.

SIR HENRY TAYLOR

Leaving a Legacy

MY HEART IS STEADFAST, O GOD;
I WILL SING AND MAKE MUSIC
WITH ALL MY SOUL.

PSALM 108:1

William Congreve said, "Music alone with sudden charms can bind the wand'ring sense, and calm the troubled mind." Walter Turnbull, founder of the Boys Choir of Harlem, would add that music can also change the life of a child.

The success of Turnbull's work is well documented. An astounding 98 percent of his choir members finish high school and go on to college. More important, they benefit from Turnbull's teachings. A healthy dose of old-fashioned values is mixed in with the music he teaches—the kind of values Turnbull learned as a child in rural Mississippi.

He believes America's sense of community is slipping away, and he hopes to impress upon his choir members the importance of nurturing one another to excel. For twenty-six years, Turnbull has demonstrated this principle to his students by taking them around the world—to Europe, Japan, Canada, and the Caribbean.

With a current roster of 450 boys and girls, eight to eighteen years old, that's no small feat. But numbers and age do not matter to Turnbull. Character does. His satisfaction comes from knowing that his choir members are learning to be better people.

Most of us would love to leave the kind of legacy Walter Turnbull is leaving to the world. What we need to recognize is that Turnbull didn't create his 450-member choir in a day. He started where he was with a small group of neighborhood kids in a church basement. He didn't have money for choir robes or music. But he did have a desire to introduce those children to the joy of music.

Do what you can, where you are, with the people God has placed in your path right now, especially your students. Regardless of how you help others, you *will* put a song in their hearts.

NOTHING GREAT WAS
EVER DONE WITHOUT
MUCH ENDURING.

CATHERINE OF SIENA

THE BIG PICTURE

During World War II, parachutes were constructed by the thousands in factories across the United States. From the worker's point of view, the job was tedious. It required stitching endless lengths of colorless fabric, crouched over a sewing machine eight to ten hours a day. The result of a day's work was a formless, massive heap of cloth that had no *visible* resemblance to a parachute.

To keep the workers motivated and concerned with quality, the management in one factory held a meeting with its workers each morning. The workers were told approximately how many parachutes had been strapped onto the backs of pilots, copilots, and other "flying" personnel the previous day. They knew just how many men had jumped to safety from disabled planes. The managers encouraged their workers to see the "big picture" of their job.

> "I GO TO PREPARE A PLACE FOR YOU. AND IF I GO AND PREPARE A PLACE FOR YOU, I WILL COME AGAIN AND RECEIVE YOU TO MYSELF; THAT WHERE I AM, THERE YOU MAY BE ALSO."
>
> JOHN 14:2-3 NKJV

As a second means of motivation, the workers were asked to form a mental picture of a husband, brother, or son who might be the one saved by the parachute they were sewing.

The level of quality in that factory was one of the highest on record![22]

Don't let the tedium of each day's chores and responsibilities wear you down, so you only see the "stitching" in front of you. Keep your eyes on the big picture. Focus on *why* you do what you do and who will benefit from your work, including those you don't know and may never meet. You may not have all the answers to the question, "Why am I here?" but you can rest assured, the Lord does!

Ultimately, the Bible tells us we will be in Heaven for eternity—and that is the biggest picture of all! God is preparing us for Heaven, just as He is preparing Heaven for us. He is creating us to be the people He wants to live with forever.

Today as you face your students, see them in the light of eternity. Teaching will take on a whole new meaning!

IT IS OUR BEST WORK THAT GOD WANTS, NOT THE DREGS OF OUR EXHAUSTION. I THINK HE MUST PREFER QUALITY TO QUANTITY.

GEORGE MACDONALD

TAPROOTS

The art of raising miniature trees, known as bonsai, was developed by the Japanese. To create a miniature tree, the taproot is cut, forcing the tree to live on only the nourishment provided by the little roots growing along the surface of the soil. The tree lives, but it does not grow. Trees dwarfed in this way reach a height of only twelve to eighteen inches.

The taproot of a tree is the part of the root system that goes deep into the soil to absorb essential minerals and huge quantities of water—sometimes several hundred quarts a day. Taproots grow deepest in dry, sandy areas where there is little rainfall. The root system of a tree not only nourishes the tree but provides stability, anchoring it securely into the ground, so it can not be blown over by strong winds.

The root system is a good analogy for the Christian life. Richard J. Foster wrote, "Superficiality is the curse of our age. . . . The desperate need today is not for a greater number of intelligent people or gifted people, but for deep people."

THE ALMIGHTY . . . BLESSES YOU WITH BLESSINGS OF THE HEAVENS ABOVE [AND] BLESSINGS OF THE DEEP THAT LIES BELOW.

GENESIS 49:25

How do Christians grow deep in their spiritual lives? In the same way a taproot grows deep—in search of the nourishment that will cause it to grow. In modern culture, Christians have to seek out spiritual food that will result in spiritual maturity. Regular times of prayer and Bible study, individual and corporate worship, serving others, and Christian fellowship are just some of the ways Christians can grow deep roots.

What are the benefits of depth in our spiritual lives? Like the tree:

- we will be able to stand strong—"the righteous cannot be uprooted" (Proverbs 12:3), and

- we will be fruitful—"the root of the righteous flourishes" (Proverbs 12:12).

Seek the Lord daily, so you can grow *deep* in your faith and bear much fruit for Him.

ONE DROP OF GOD'S STRENGTH IS
WORTH MORE THAN ALL THE WORLD.

DWIGHT LYMAN MOODY

WHAT ARE YOU DOING TODAY?

PRAISE THE LORD, ALL YOU GENTILES!
LAUD HIM, ALL YOU PEOPLES! FOR
HIS MERCIFUL KINDNESS IS GREAT
TOWARD US. AND THE TRUTH OF
THE LORD ENDURES FOREVER.

PSALM 117:1-2 NKJV

In the Middle Ages a man was sent to a building site in France to see how the workers felt about their labor. He approached the first worker and asked, "What are you doing?"

The worker snapped at him, "Are you blind? I'm cutting these impossible boulders with primitive tools and putting them together the way the boss tells me. I'm sweating under this hot sun. My back is breaking. I'm bored. I make next to nothing!"

The man quickly backed away and found a second worker to whom he asked the same question, "What are you doing?"

The second worker replied, "I'm shaping these boulders into useable forms. Then they are put together according to the architect's plans. I earn five francs a week, and that supports my wife and family. It's a job. Could be worse."

A little encouraged but not overwhelmed by this response, the man went to yet a third worker. "What are you doing?" he asked.

"Why, can't you see?" the worker said as he lifted his arm to the sky. "I'm building a cathedral!"[23]

How we regard our work may not affect whether a task gets done or not. It will, however, have an impact on the quality of our work and our productivity. Those who see value in their jobs enjoy a greater sense of purpose.

Any job can be done with grace, dignity, style, and purpose; you only have to choose to see it that way!

IF YOUR DAILY LIFE SEEMS POOR, DO NOT BLAME IT; BLAME YOURSELF, TELL YOURSELF THAT YOU ARE NOT POET ENOUGH TO CALL FORTH ITS RICHES.

RAINER MARIA RILKE

THE VALUE OF ONE

Some days it's hard just to get out of bed. Our motivation is fading or completely gone. We are overcome with a "What difference does it make?" attitude. We become overwhelmed at the enormity of the duties before us. Our talents and resources seem minuscule in comparison to the task.

"THERE IS JOY IN THE PRESENCE OF THE ANGELS OF GOD OVER ONE SINNER WHO REPENTS."

LUKE 15:10 NASB

A businessman and his wife once took a much-needed getaway at an oceanside hotel. During their stay a powerful storm arose, lashing the beach and sending massive breakers against the shore. The storm woke the man. He lay still in bed listening to the storm's fury and reflecting on his own life of constant and continual demands and pressures.

Before daybreak the wind subsided. The man got out of bed to go outside and survey the damage done by the storm. He walked along the beach and noticed it was covered with starfish that had been thrown ashore by the massive waves. They were lying helplessly on the sandy beach. Unable to get to the water, the starfish faced inevitable death as the sun's rays dried them out.

Down the beach, the man saw a figure walking along the shore. The figure would stoop and pick something up. In the dim of the early-morning twilight, he couldn't quite make it all out. As he approached he realized it was a young boy picking up the starfish one at a time and flinging them back into the ocean to safety.

As the man neared the young boy he said, "Why are you doing that? One person will never make a difference—there are too many starfish to get back into the water before the sun comes up."

The boy said sadly, "Yes, that's true," and then bent to pick up another starfish. Then he said, "But I can sure make a difference to that one."

God never intended for an individual to solve all of life's problems. But He did intend for each one of us to use whatever resources and gifts He gave us to make a difference where we arc.[24]

DO WHAT YOU CAN, WITH WHAT
YOU HAVE, WHERE YOU ARE.

THEODORE ROOSEVELT

A CORK'S INFLUENCE

A tour group passed through a particular room in a factory. They viewed an elongated bar of steel, which weighed five hundred pounds, suspended vertically by a chain. Near it, an average-size cork was suspended by a silk thread.

"You will see something shortly which is seemingly impossible," said an attendant to the group of sightseers. "This cork is going to set this steel bar in motion!"

She took the cork in her hand, pulled it only slightly to the side of its original position, and released it. The cork swung gently against the steel bar, which remained motionless.

For ten minutes the cork, with pendulum-like regularity, struck the iron bar. Finally, the bar vibrated slightly. By the time the tour group passed through the room an hour later, the great bar was swinging like the pendulum of a clock!

Many of us feel we are not exerting a feather's weight of influence upon others or making a dent in the bastions of evil in the world. Not so! Sometimes we don't realize how powerful the cumulative influence of God's goodness, which we walk in, is to those around us.

Not everyone is called to spread the love of Jesus through the pulpit, on the evangelistic trail, or in a full-time counseling ministry. Most of us are called to live our lives as "corks," through word and example—quietly, gently tapping away through the work of our daily lives. Tap by loving tap, in God's time, even the quietest Christian can make a huge difference in the lives of those whom preachers may never reach.

As you go about your day today, remember that even a smile can warm a students' hearts and draw them to Jesus.

THE GREATEST THING A MAN
CAN DO FOR HIS HEAVENLY
FATHER IS TO BE KIND TO SOME
OF HIS OTHER CHILDREN.

HENRY DRUMMOND

EVENING AND MORNING

THERE WAS EVENING, AND THERE WAS MORNING—THE FIRST DAY.

GENESIS 1:5

In the Book of Genesis, each day of creation is concluded with the phrase, "and there was evening, and there was morning."

From the Hebrew perspective, the day begins at evening, specifically with the setting of the sun. How unlike our Western tradition, where we start our days at the crack of dawn and consider night to be the end of a long day.

What does it mean for the day to begin at evening?

For Hebrew people through the centuries, the transition from afternoon to evening has been marked by prayer. "Evening prayer" is a Jewish custom. After prayer, families gather together for a meal.

The most holy day of the week, the Sabbath, begins with the lighting of candles and a proclamation of faith, then a more formal family dinner. After the evening meal, Jewish families traditionally gather together to read God's Word and discuss how His laws apply to their lives. The evening ends in rest.

Consider the priorities evidenced by their way of life:

First, a focus upon prayer and one's relationship with God.

Second, an emphasis on family life.

Third, a daily study of Scripture, making God's Word the last thoughts of the day.

Fourth, rest and sleep.

It was only after a Hebrew talked with God, enjoyed the love and fellowship of family, studied the Scriptures, and rested, that work was undertaken!

Why not give it a try? Begin your next day in the evening, and wake up knowing you're totally refreshed—spirit, soul, and body—to have a full and productive day!

THE BIBLE IS MEANT TO
BE BREAD FOR OUR DAILY
USE, NOT JUST CAKE FOR
SPECIAL OCCASIONS.

ANONYMOUS

QUALITY TIME

Busy—so busy! The sun has long since set and there is still so much to do. Work, family, church, and much more seem to demand hours God never put in the day. Still, we Christians think all these accomplishments will please our Heavenly Father. After all, faith without works is dead, right?

When we finally fall into bed at night, can we say we've actually spent any time with the Father we're trying so hard to please?

In his book, *Unto the Hills,* Billy Graham tells a story about a little girl and her father who were great friends and enjoyed spending time together. They went for walks and shared a passion for watching birds, enjoying the changing seasons, and meeting people who crossed their path.

One day, the father noticed a change in his daughter. If he went for a walk, she excused herself from going. Knowing she was growing up, he rationalized that she must be expected to lose interest in her daddy as she made other friends. Nevertheless, her absence grieved him deeply.

Because of his daughter's absences, he was not in a particularly happy mood on his birthday. Then she presented him with a pair of exquisitely worked slippers, which she had hand made for him while he was out of the house walking.

At last he understood and said, "My darling, I like these slippers very much, but next time buy the slippers and let me have you all the days. I would rather have you than anything you can make for me."[25]

Is it possible our Heavenly Father sometimes feels lonely for the company of His children? Are we so busy doing good that we forget—or are we too weary—to spend some quiet time with Him as our day draws to a close?

Take a walk with your Heavenly Father as the sun sets. Spend some quality time, talking to Him about anything and everything. You will be blessed, and so will He!

WE ARE NOT FORCED TO TAKE
WINGS TO FIND HIM, BUT HAVE
ONLY TO SEEK SOLITUDE AND TO
LOOK WITHIN OURSELVES. YOU
NEED NOT BE OVERWHELMED WITH
CONFUSION BEFORE SO KIND A GUEST,
BUT WITH UTTER HUMILITY, TALK TO
HIM AS TO YOUR FATHER; ASK FOR
WHAT YOU WANT AS FROM A FATHER.

SAINT TERESA OF AVILA

FINAL MEDITATION

One of the translations for the word *meditate* in Hebrew, the language in which the Old Testament was written, is the verb "to mutter"—to voice under one's breath, to continually repeat something. When we are taught to meditate upon the Lord and His Word day and night, we are to repeat God's Word to ourselves continually. When we do this, God's Word becomes foremost in our thinking. It becomes our mind-set, our world view, our perspective on life.

The Scriptures promise that when we think and speak in accordance with God's law, we will act accordingly. Thus we will enjoy success and prosperity!

In the opinion of Henry Ward Beecher, a great preacher from the 1800s, "A few moments with God at that calm and tranquil season, are of more value than much fine gold."

The psalmist proclaimed, "My mouth shall praise thee with joyful lips: when I remember thee upon my bed, and meditate on thee in the night watches" (Psalm 63:5-6 KJV).

Let God's Word be your last conscious thought before sleeping. Turn off the late show, close the novel, put away the work, and rest in the Lord, recalling His Word. You'll find it easier to do this if you choose a passage of Scripture on which to meditate in the morning and then meditate upon it all day—muttering phrases and verses to yourself in the odd moments of your schedule. Then, just before you fall asleep, remind yourself one final time of God's truth.

Those who do this report a more restful night. A peaceful mind focused on God's Word seems to produce peaceful sleep and deep relaxation for the body. In this day and age, with nearly a billion dollars spent each year on sleep aids, we have the greatest sleep aid of all— the Word of God!

MEDITATION IS THE SOUL'S CHEWING.

WILLIAM GRIMSHAW

HIS PROMISE OF PEACE

BE STILL, AND KNOW THAT I AM GOD.

PSALM 46:10 KJV

A woman who grew up on a large farm in Pennsylvania fondly remembers some special times with her father. Because the growing and harvest seasons were pretty much over from November through March, she recalls thinking that her father set aside that time each year just to be with her.

"During the winter months," she says, "Dad didn't have to work as hard and long as he did the rest of the year. In fact, it seemed like there were some times when he didn't work at all as far as I could tell.

"During those long winter months, he had a habit of sitting by the fire. He never refused my bid to climb up on his lap, and he rewarded my effort by holding me close for hours at a time. Often, he would read to me or invite me to read a story to him. Sometimes I would fall asleep as we talked about all the things that are important to dads and little girls. Other times, we didn't talk at all. We just gazed at the fire and enjoyed the warmth of our closeness. Oh, how I treasured those intimate moments.

"As I grew, I thought it odd that other kids dreaded the 'indoor' days of winter. For me they meant the incredible pleasure of having my father very nearly all to myself."[26]

Just as winter is God's season of rest for the earth, we sometimes experience "winter" in our spiritual lives. The world may seem a cold place. Like children who dread "indoor days," we can feel stifled and penned in by these spiritual winters.

If you are going through a dry, wintry time, why not snuggle close to the Heavenly Father tonight and listen to His gentle voice? The love and comfort He wants to give you will surely warm your heart!

A GREAT MANY PEOPLE ARE TRYING TO MAKE PEACE, BUT THAT HAS ALREADY BEEN DONE. GOD HAS NOT LEFT IT FOR US TO DO; ALL WE HAVE TO DO IS TO ENTER INTO IT.

DWIGHT LYMAN MOODY

FRAGMENTS

Margaret Brownley tells of her son's first letters from camp: "When my oldest son went away to summer camp for the first time, I was a nervous wreck. Although he was nine years old, he hadn't as much as spent a night away from home, let alone an entire week. I packed his suitcase with special care, making sure he had enough socks and underwear to see him through the week. I also packed stationery and stamps so he could write home.

ONE DAY JESUS WAS PRAYING IN A CERTAIN PLACE. WHEN HE FINISHED, ONE OF HIS DISCIPLES SAID TO HIM, "LORD TEACH US TO PRAY."

LUKE 11:1

"I received the first letter from him three days after he left for camp. I quickly tore open the envelope and stared at the childish scrawl, which read: *Camp is fun, but the food is yucky!* The next letter offered little more: *Jerry wet the bed.* 'Who's Jerry?' I wondered. The third and final letter had this interesting piece of news: *The nurse said it's not broken.*

"Fragments. Bits of information that barely skim the surface. A preview of coming attractions that never materialize. It made me think of my own sparse messages to God. 'Dear Lord,' I plead when a son is late coming home, 'keep him safe.' Or, 'Give me strength,' I pray when faced with a difficult neighbor or the challenge of a checkbook run amuck. 'Let me have wisdom,' is another favorite prayer of mine, usually murmured in haste while waiting my turn at a parent/teacher conference or dealing with a difficult employee. 'Thank-you, God,' I say before each meal or when my brood is tucked in safely for the night.

"Fragments. Bits and pieces. Are my messages to God as unsatisfactory to Him as my son's letters were to me? With a guilty start, I realized that it had been a long time since I'd had a meaningful chat with the Lord.

"When my son came home, he told me all about his adventures. It was good to have him home and safe. 'Thank-you, God,' I murmured, and then caught myself. It was time I sent God more than just a hasty note from 'camp.'"[27]

A SINGLE GRATEFUL THOUGHT
RAISED TO HEAVEN IS THE
MOST PERFECT PRAYER.

GOTTHOLD EPHRAIM LESSING

ALL THE DETAILS

Andrea was in no mood for her six-year-old son's Saturday morning antics. While Steven argued with his friends over video games, Andrea stewed over her own mounting pile of pressures. Just-bought groceries for tomorrow's dinner guests sprawled across every bit of counter space. Buried under them was a Sunday-school lesson to be prepared. A week's worth of laundry spilled out of the laundry room into the kitchen, and an upsetting letter from a faraway friend in need lay teetering on the edge of the sink.

In the midst of this turmoil, Steven's Sunday-school teacher called. "Is Steven going to the carnival with us this afternoon?"

"He didn't mention anything about it."

"DO NOT LET YOUR HEARTS BE TROUBLED. TRUST IN GOD; TRUST ALSO IN ME."

JOHN 14:1

"Well, we'll be leaving about noon. If he didn't bring home his permission slip, just write the usual information on a slip of paper and send it along with him." As soon as Andrea reminded Steven about the trip, his mood changed and he was his "better self" for the next couple of hours.

Andrea was just pulling a cake from the oven when she heard the doorbell ring, followed by an awful commotion. Rushing to the living room she found two little girls waving pink slips of paper at her crying son. "What's the matter?" she asked as she gently put her arms around him.

"I can't go!" he wailed. "I don't have one of those pink papers!"

"Oh, yes you do. Only yours happens to be white," she said as she dried his tears, stuffed the paper into his pocket, and sent him out the door.

Back in the kitchen Andrea wondered, "Why didn't he just ask me about the paper? Hasn't he been my child long enough to know I'd have a solution?"

Suddenly a tiny smile crept across her face as she surveyed the chaos around her—and she could almost hear her Heavenly Father say, "Haven't you been My child long enough to know that I have it taken care of?"[28]

IF WE LOVE CHRIST MUCH, SURELY
WE SHALL TRUST HIM MUCH.

THOMAS BENTON BROOKS

HEAVEN'S SPOT REMOVER

IT IS OF THE LORD'S MERCIES THAT WE ARE
NOT CONSUMED, BECAUSE HIS COM-
PASSIONS FAIL NOT. THEY ARE NEW EVERY
MORNING: GREAT IS THY FAITHFULNESS.

LAMENTATIONS 3:22-23 KJV

"Let it snow, let it snow, let it snow." That's the cry of school-aged children everywhere when winter weather finally arrives.

First, there's catching those early snowflakes on your tongue. After a few more flakes hit the ground, you can start making snowballs and have some terrific battles. Several inches later, it's time to build the snowmen and snow forts. And when the blanket of snow reaches a hefty thickness, the best thing to do is make snow angels.

Remember snow angels? You find a good patch of untouched snow, stand with your arms stretched out to the side, and fall backwards onto what feels like a cold, wet cloud. Stay on your back for a few moments and stare at the sky. When the cold starts getting to you, flap your arms and legs as if you're doing jumping jacks. Then, carefully get up and look at your handiwork.

Between the snowballs and snowmen, the forts and the angels, it isn't long before every square inch of clean snow has been used up. Patches of dead grass show through where someone dug down deep to roll a snowman's head. The once-pristine landscape is now trampled and rutted.

But something magical happens overnight. While you are sleeping, the snow falls again. You look out your window in the morning to find another clean white blanket covering all of the previous day's blemishes. All that was ugly is once again beautiful.

Don't despair when what began as a beautiful day turns into something ugly. The God who turned the humiliation and shame of His Son's death on the cross into the gift of salvation can take the tattered rags of our daily lives and make them like new again—every morning.

IF GOD MAINTAINS
SUN AND PLANETS IN
BRIGHT AND ORDERED
BEAUTY HE CAN KEEP US.

F. B. MEYER

WILDFLOWER WORTH

Each spring, wildflowers bloom in profusion at a place in Idaho called "Craters of the Moon." Nourished by snowmelt and occasional rains, the flowers spring up in the lava rock left by an eons-old volcano. It is a stunning sight to see the small, delicate wildflower blossoms bursting into life amid the huge, rugged boulders.

Sightseers can follow footpaths all through the lava rocks to discover the surprising spots that dusty maiden, dwarf monkey flower, and Indian paintbrush find to grow. The life span for the fragile flowers can be as brief as one day if the hot desert winds blow into the area. Even without the winds, three weeks is about their longest show.

When Jesus taught His followers, He often sat outside. Perhaps He sat among the spring wildflowers when He pointed at the lilies, encouraging the worriers not to be blinded to the fact that God takes care of all

"LOOK AT THE LILIES AND HOW THEY GROW. THEY DON'T WORK, YET SOLOMON IN ALL HIS GLORY WAS NOT DRESSED AS BEAUTIFULLY AS THEY ARE. AND IF GOD CARES SO WONDERFULLY FOR FLOWERS, WON'T HE MORE SURELY CARE FOR YOU?"

LUKE 12:27-28 NLT

His creation, even a short-lived wildflower. If He takes care of them, He certainly will care for us.

How do we avoid worry? By increasing our faith in our God who loves us. By starting each day focusing on Him instead of our fears and remembering His loving care, even for the brief life of a wildflower.

ALL I COULD NEVER BE,
ALL MEN IGNORED IN ME—
THIS, I WAS WORTH TO GOD.

ROBERT BROWNING

THE SUNSET DECISION

Jenny Lind, known as "The Swedish Nightingale," won worldwide success as a talented opera singer. She sang for heads of state in many nations and thrilled hundreds of thousands of people in an era when all performances were live.

Not only did her fame grow, but her fortune increased as well. Yet at the height of her career, at a time when her voice was at its peak, she left the stage and never returned.

She must have missed the fame, the money, and the applause of thousands—or so her fans surmised—but Jenny Lind was content to live in quiet seclusion with her husband.

Once an English friend went to visit her. He found her on the beach with a Bible on her knee. As he approached, he saw that her attention was fixed upon a magnificent sunset.

They talked of old days and former acquaintances, and eventually the conversation turned to her new life. "How is it that you came to abandon the stage at the apex of your career?"

Jenny offered a quiet answer that reflected her peace of heart: "When every day, it made me think less of this (laying a finger on the Bible) and nothing at all of that (pointing to the sunset), what else could I do?"

Has a busy, successful life robbed you of some of the most precious gifts of God? Next time you miss a sunset or prayer time because of a crowded schedule, remember Jenny's priorities.

Nothing in life is as precious as your relationship with your Heavenly Father, and then your relationships with family members and friends. Ultimate fulfillment comes not in career or money, but in relationship with God and others.

THE GREAT USE OF LIFE IS TO SPEND IT
FOR SOMETHING THAT OUTLASTS IT.

WILLIAM JAMES

RUNNING ON EMPTY

THERE REMAINS, THEN, A SABBATH-
REST FOR THE PEOPLE OF GOD;
FOR ANYONE WHO ENTERS GOD'S REST
ALSO RESTS FROM HIS OWN WORK,
JUST AS GOD DID FROM HIS.

HEBREWS 4:9-10

Some years ago, a research physician made an extensive study of the amount of oxygen a person needs throughout the day. He was able to demonstrate that the average workman breathes thirty ounces of oxygen during a day's work, but he uses thirty-one. At the close of the day, he is one ounce short and his body is tired.

He goes to sleep and breathes more oxygen than he uses to sleep, so in the morning he has regained five-sixths of the ounce he was short. But the night's rest does not fully balance the day's work!

By the seventh day, he is six-sixths—or one whole ounce—in debt again. He must rest an entire day to replenish his body's oxygen requirements.

Further, he demonstrated that replenishing an entire ounce of oxygen requires thirty to thirty-six hours (one twenty-four-hour day plus the preceding and following nights) when part of the resting is done while one is awake and moving about.

Over time, failure to replenish the oxygen supply results in the actual death of cells and, eventually, the premature death of the person.

A person is restored as long as he or she takes the seventh day as a day of rest.[29]

Most people think that "keeping the Sabbath" is solely an act of devotion to God. But in turning your attention to Him, He can offer you true rest and replenishment in every area of your life—spirit, soul, *and* body. He is not only our daily strength, He is our source of rest, recreation, and replenishment.

YOU WILL BREAK THE
BOW IF YOU KEEP IT
ALWAYS BENT.

GREEK PROVERB

FIVE MINUTES

If you wake up as weary as you were when you went to bed the night before, try to recall what you were thinking about during the last five minutes before you went to sleep. What you think about in that five minutes impacts how well you sleep, which determines what kind of day the following day will be.

When you sleep, your conscious mind is at rest, but your subconscious mind remains active. Psychologists call the subconscious the "assistant manager of life." When the conscious mind is "off duty," the subconscious mind takes over. The subconscious carries out the orders that are given to it, even though you are not aware of it.

> IN PEACE I WILL BOTH LIE DOWN AND SLEEP; FOR THOU ALONE, O LORD, MAKEST ME DWELL IN SAFETY.
>
> PSALM 4:8 RSV

For example, if the last minutes before going to sleep are spent worrying, the subconscious records and categorizes that as fear and acts as if the fear is reality. Thus muscles remain tense, nerves are on edge, and the body's organs are upset, which means the body is not really at rest.

However, if those last five minutes are spent contemplating some great idea, an inspiring verse, or a calm and reassuring thought, it will signal to the nervous system, "All is well," and put the entire body in a relaxed, peaceful state. This helps you to wake up refreshed, strengthened, and confident.

Many of the days that begin badly started out that way because of the night before, during those critical last five minutes of conscious thought. You can input positive, healthy thoughts into your conscious mind and pave the way for quiet, restful sleep by simply meditating on God's Word as you drop off to sleep. For example, Psalm 91:1-2 (NKJV):

> He who dwells in the secret place of the Most High shall abide under the shadow of the Almighty. I will say of the Lord, "He is my refuge and my fortress; my God, in Him I will trust."

Sweet dreams!

TIRED NATURE'S SWEET RESTORER,

BALMY SLEEP!

EDWARD YOUNG

SHINING THROUGH

A little girl was among a group of people being given a guided tour through a great cathedral. As the guide explained the various parts of the structure—the altar, the choir, the screen, and the nave—the little girl's attention was intently focused on a stained-glass window.

For a long time she silently pondered the window. Looking up at the various figures, her face was bathed in a rainbow of color as the afternoon sun poured into the transept of the huge cathedral.

"LET YOUR LIGHT SO SHINE BEFORE MEN, THAT THEY MAY SEE YOUR GOOD WORKS AND GLORIFY YOUR FATHER IN HEAVEN."

MATTHEW 5:16 NKJV

As the group was about to move on, she gathered enough courage to ask the tour conductor a question. "Who are those people in that pretty window?"

"Those are the saints," the guide replied.

That night, as the little girl was preparing for bed, she told her mother proudly: "I know who the saints are."

"Oh?" replied the mother. "And just who *are* the saints?"

Without a moment's hesitation the little girl replied: "They are the people who let the light shine through!"[30]

As you look back over your day, did you let God's light shine through? Sometimes we pass these opportunities by saying, "It will just take too much out of me." But the Bible lets us know that everything we give will come back to us—multiplied (Luke 6:38 KJV).

We see this principle in nature. A microscopic speck of radium can send out a stream of sparks which give off light and heat, yet in emitting the light and heat, it does not deplete itself of its own energy.

As Christians we are called to share the light of Jesus in a world of darkness. Like rays of light that break through gloom and darkness, we can bring hope and encouragement.

Remember, the light of your life gives those around you a glimpse of Jesus, the Source of eternal and constant light. As you let your light shine, it will grow brighter!

SHOULD FIRST MY LAMP SPREAD LIGHT
AND PUREST RAYS BESTOW
THE OIL MUST THEN FROM YOU,
MY DEAREST JESUS, FLOW.

ANGELUS SILESIUS

A HINT OF ETERNITY

WE FIX OUR EYES NOT ON WHAT
IS SEEN, BUT ON WHAT IS UNSEEN.
FOR WHAT IS SEEN IS TEMPORARY,
BUT WHAT IS UNSEEN IS ETERNAL.

2 CORINTHIANS 4:18

Eternity is a difficult concept for us to grasp. In human terms, it seems a matter of time—or more accurately, timelessness. But eternity is more than a measure of time. Things said to be "eternal" have a quality of permanence. The benefits of eternal things are not found solely in the hereafter; they provide an incredible sense of satisfaction in this life as well.

The late Lorado Taft, one of America's great artists, often said that a real work of art must have in it "a hint of eternity." The writer of Ecclesiastes says that God has not only made everything beautiful, but He has set eternity in the hearts of men (Ecclesiastes 3:11). When we do good work, whether it is in the classroom or not, we may find in it a hint of eternity, the abiding value that outlasts silver or gold.

Daniel Webster, one of America's most famous statesmen, once said: "If we work on marble, it will perish; if on brass, time will efface it; if we rear temples, they will crumble into dust; but if we work on immortal souls and imbue them with principles, with the just fear of God and love of our fellowmen, we engrave on those tablets something that will brighten to all eternity."

Ascending to the top of one of the magnificent stairways in the Library of Congress, one reads this inscription on the wall: "Too low they build who build beneath the stars."

In building your life, build with God toward everlasting life. In building your students, build to the glory of Jesus Christ and invest in their eternity.

ETERNITY HAS NO GRAY HAIRS! THE FLOWERS FADE, THE HEART WITHERS, MAN GROWS OLD AND DIES, THE WORLD LIES DOWN IN THE SEPULCHRE OF AGES, BUT TIME WRITES NO WRINKLES ON THE BROW OF ETERNITY.

REGINALD HEBER

OUT OF SIGHT

A tree is nothing without its roots, and for the most part they do their job underground. Young roots absorb water and minerals from the soil. Older roots take these materials and send them into the stem.

In order to keep the tree going during dormant periods, the roots store food, similar to the way a bear builds bulk to get him through hibernation. Food stored in the tree's roots provides energy and food needed when the weather changes and it's time for new growth.

Trees never stop growing. As long as they live, some type of growth is taking place. New roots are forming, new branches are appearing, or old bark is being sloughed off so that new bark can take its place. Without the roots to lend mechanical support, act as anchors, and store food, a tree would fall.

The God who cares enough about trees to set up an intricate feeding system for them gives each of us the food, water,

JUST AS YOU RECEIVED CHRIST JESUS AS LORD, CONTINUE TO LIVE IN HIM, ROOTED AND BUILT UP IN HIM, STRENGTHENED IN THE FAITH AS YOU WERE TAUGHT, AND OVERFLOWING WITH THANKFULNESS.

COLOSSIANS 2:6-7

and air we require to survive. He gives us family and friends, opportunities, and provision to accomplish His plan for our lives. We can't see God with our physical eyes, but like the finely developed web of roots beneath the ground, we know He's there, working on our behalf. That is His nature as Jehovah Jireh—the God who provides.

Have you ever been hungry? Jesus is the bread of life; He promises that whoever comes to Him will never go hungry (John 6:35 KJV).

Have you ever been thirsty? As Jesus told the Samaritan woman at the well, "Whoever drinks the water I give him will never thirst" (John 4:14).

Do you ever find yourself gasping for breath? Job knew who to thank for the air we all breathe. "In his hand is the life of every creature and the breath of all mankind" (Job 12:10).

STAY ROOTED IN THE LORD AND WATCH HIM PROVIDE FOR YOUR EVERY NEED! HE THAT SO MUCH FOR YOU DID DO, WILL DO YET MORE.

THOMAS WASHBOURNE

FINISHING WELL

Putting the finish on a piece of furniture is the final step in its construction. The bulk of the work that gives the chest, table, or chair its *function* happens much earlier in the process. But it is the finish—the staining and varnishing—that very often gives a piece of furniture its *beauty*. The finish brings out the grain and luster of the wood, the smoothness of the craftsmanship, and the shine that speaks of completion.

The cross on which Jesus was crucified marked the end of His earthly life. As He exhaled His last breath, He declared, "It is finished." This was a triumphant statement that marked the completion of His earthly mission to satisfy and fulfill God's law for all mankind. The Cross became the beacon that shines brightly into sinful hearts and says, "You can be free." It also became the prelude for a "new beginning" at His resurrection—offering new life for all.

AS HE HAD BEGUN, SO HE WOULD ALSO COMPLETE THIS GRACE IN YOU.

2 CORINTHIANS 8:6

NKJV

We are each called to end our lives well, but our finish is not simply at our death. It is also in our bringing closure to each day in such a way that we allow for our resurrection the following morning. It is saying with thankfulness and humility, "To the best of my ability, I've done what the Lord put before me to do today. And now, I give my all to Him anew so that He might recreate me and use me again tomorrow."

Ralph Waldo Emerson offered this advice: "Finish every day and be done with it. You have done what you could. Some blunders and absurdities no doubt crept in; forget them as soon as you can. Tomorrow is a new day; begin it well and serenely and with too high a spirit to be cumbered with your old nonsense. This day is all that is good and fair. It is too dear, with its hopes and invitations, to waste a moment on yesterdays."

Amen! The God who began a good work in you, will finish it day by day, and ultimately bring it to completion (Philippians 1:6 KJV).

LET EACH MAN THINK HIMSELF AN
ACT OF GOD, HIS MIND A THOUGHT
OF GOD, HIS LIFE A BREATH OF GOD.

PHILIP JAMES BAILEY

LISTEN FOR THE MUSIC

HOW SHALL WE SING THE LORD'S
SONG IN A STRANGE LAND?

PSALM 137:4 KJV

George Gershwin was talking to a friend on the crowded beach of a resort near New York City when the joyous shrieks of voices pierced their conversation. Clanking tunes ground out from a nearby merry-go-round, while barkers and hucksters shouted themselves hoarse. From underground came the deep roar of the subway; beside them crashed the relentless waves of the ocean.

Gershwin listened and then remarked to his friend, "All of this could form such a beautiful pattern of sound. It could turn into a magnificent musical piece expressive of every human activity and feeling with pauses, counterpoints, blends and climaxes of sound that would be beautiful. . . . But it is not that. . . . It is all discordant, terrible and exhausting—as we hear it now. The pattern is always being shattered."

What a parable of our time! So many confusing sounds and noises, so much unrest, so much rapid change. But somewhere in the midst of it, a pattern could emerge; a meaning could come out of it.

Our job is to hear the music in the noise.

Sometimes, finding the melodic line is a simple matter of listening selectively—mentally tuning out all but one sound for a while. That's what happens when we sit for a few minutes over a cup of tea and listen intently to that coworker, student, or friend. Once we listen and truly hear the "tune" they're playing, their unique melody will always be distinct to us, even in the cacophony of busy days.

If we are intentional about what we hear, the conflicting chaos swirling around our own symphony will be weeded out; God's music will be easier to hear.

This afternoon take time to be a creative listener!

I HAVE SHOWN YOU THE
POWER OF SILENCE, HOW
THOROUGHLY IT HEALS AND
HOW FULLY PLEASING IT IS
TO GOD. . . . IT IS BY SILENCE
THAT THE SAINTS GREW. . . .
IT WAS BECAUSE OF SILENCE
THAT THE POWER OF GOD
DWELT IN THEM; BECAUSE
OF SILENCE THAT THE
MYSTERIES OF GOD WERE
KNOWN TO THEM.

FATHER AMMONAS

PASS IT ON!

On the first day of his cruise in the Caribbean, a man entering his senior years noticed an attractive woman about his age. She gave him a friendly smile as he passed her on the deck.

That evening at dinner, he was seated at the same table with her. To make conversation, he commented that he had appreciated her kind smile during his afternoon walk. When she heard this, she said, "The reason I smiled was that when I saw you, I was immediately struck by your strong resemblance to my third husband."

"Oh," he said. "How many times have you been married?" he asked with interest.

She looked down at her dinner plate, a slight smile crossed her face, and she tentatively answered, "Twice."

OUR MOUTH WAS FILLED WITH LAUGHTER, AND OUR TONGUE WITH SHOUTS OF JOY.

PSALM 126:2 RSV

A smile is a great encourager!

An unknown author said it well:

A smile costs nothing, but gives much. It enriches those who receive, without making poorer those who give. It takes but a moment, but the memory of it sometimes lasts forever. None is so rich or mighty that they can get along without it, and none is so poor but that they can be made rich by it.

A smile creates happiness in the home, fosters good will in business, and is the countersign of friendship. It brings rest to the weary, cheer to the discouraged, sunshine to the sad, and it is nature's antidote for trouble.

Have you been grumpy today? Ask God for a double dose of His joy, and then put a smile on your face. Let people, including your students, know you refuse to take on the negativism or cynicism of the world. You can be cheerful and pass that cheer on to others with a simple smile.

KEEP WHAT IS WORTH KEEPING—
AND WITH A BREATH OF KINDNESS
BLOW THE REST AWAY.

DINAH MARIA MULOCK CRAIK

Sugar or Lemon?

Weekends are traditionally a time for reflecting on the work week and chatting with friends. Perhaps because we are more relaxed, we may be more careless in our conversation and include not-so-kind opinions about others.

Just as sugar and cream are slipped into the tea, verbal raspberries, lemons, and sour grapes may slip into the conversation.

Consider sharing this little poem with your friends at the beginning of your time together.

DO NOT FORGET
TO DO GOOD
AND TO SHARE
WITH OTHERS,
FOR WITH SUCH
SACRIFICES
GOD IS PLEASED.

HEBREWS 13:16 NIV

I KNOW SOMETHING GOOD ABOUT YOU

Wouldn't this world be better,
If folks whom we meet would say
"I know something good about you,"
And treat you just that way?
Wouldn't it be splendid,
If each handshake, good and true,
Carried with it this assurance:
"I know something good about you?"
Wouldn't life be happier,
If the good that's in us all,

Were the only thing about us
That people would recall?
Wouldn't our days be sweeter,
If we praised the good we see;
For there is a lot of goodness,
In the worst of you and me?
Wouldn't it be fine to practice,
This way of thinking too;
You know something good about me,
I know something good about you?

Author Unknown

GOOD WORDS ARE WORTH
MUCH AND COST LITTLE.

GEORGE HERBERT

End-of-Work Prayer

Many people are quick to pray before a meal, before they begin a new project, before they attempt something for the first time, or before embarking on a long journey. They desire to start on the right foot, asking for God's help, protection, creativity, and blessing; but what about prayer at the end of a work day, journey, or task?

Such a prayer is like a second bookend on a shelf of freestanding books—it brackets our work and brings us to full recognition that we have received from the Lord the very things we requested. Rather than being a prayer of petition, such a prayer is an expression of praise and thanksgiving.

Simeon had lived his entire life waiting to see the Messiah—a promise the Lord had made to him (Luke 2:26 KJV). Upon seeing the infant Jesus in the Temple, Simeon took Him in his arms, blessed God, and said, "Lord, now You are letting Your servant depart in peace, according to Your word; for my eyes have seen Your salvation" (Luke 2:29-30 NKJV). Simeon recognized that God had been faithful to His Word, and his heart was encouraged and filled with joy.

Simeon is a wonderful example of how we need to begin and end the events of our lives with prayer. When we reach the end of a day, haggard and weary, we can remember Simeon's prayer, "Lord, let Your servant depart in peace, according to Your Word."

Knowing God was with us today and He will be with us tomorrow, we can move on to the evening hours with freedom and a sense of satisfaction.

LET A MAN GO AWAY OR COME BACK: GOD NEVER LEAVES. HE IS ALWAYS AT HAND AND IF HE CANNOT GET INTO YOUR LIFE, STILL HE IS NEVER FARTHER AWAY THAN THE DOOR.

MEISTER ECKHART

WHAT'S THE RUSH?

Rush-hour traffic. What comes to mind when you hear those words? Chances are they don't put a smile on your face, cause your heartbeat to slow, or drop your blood pressure to healthy levels. More likely they bring up images of exhaust smoke, angry drivers, brake lights, and those ever-popular "Detour" or "Lane Closed Ahead" signs.

Rush-hour has become an oxymoron, like *jumbo shrimp*. Too many cars have taken the rush out of rush hour. Despite the number of people working part-time, on late shifts, or at home, more cars seem to be on the road between 8:00 and 9:00 A.M. and 5:00 and 6:00 P.M. than there are people on the planet. And we all know there's absolutely nothing that can be done about it—unless you live in Thailand.

> BE PATIENT, THEN, BROTHERS, UNTIL THE LORD'S COMING.
>
> JAMES 5:7

Proving that traffic cops have a sense of humor, an officer in Bangkok gave his men some rather unusual instructions. During morning rush hour at one of the worst spots in town, these traffic directors suddenly looked more like dance-troupe hopefuls than ticket-writing law enforcers.

Since the traffic wasn't going anywhere anyway, why not do some pirouettes or some break dancing? Why not smile at frustrated motorists? Why not lighten the mood (if not the load) on the road?

The result has been all they had hoped. The traffic is still tied up in knots, but people are more cheerful about their situation, and the cops are happier too.[31]

Sometimes we feel pressed on all sides, and there seems to be no way out. Perhaps those around us keep turning up the heat, and we can sense we're getting closer and closer to the breaking point.

That's when we need to realize how far we've already come and that the rest of the journey will have bright moments if we'll only reach out for them. That's the time to laugh *anyway* and do a few pirouettes!

WE MUST WAIT FOR GOD, LONG,
MEEKLY, IN THE WIND AND WET,
IN THE THUNDER AND LIGHTNING,
IN THE COLD AND THE DARK. WAIT,
AND HE WILL COME. HE NEVER COMES
TO THOSE WHO DO NOT WAIT.

FREDERICK WILLIAM FABER

OPPOSITES BALANCED

Much of our lives seem to be suspended between opposites. We grow up learning to label things as good and bad, hurtful and helpful, naughty and nice. People are kind or mean. The thermostat can be adjusted to avoid extremes of heat and cold. We look forward to the changing of seasons from summer to winter. Time is divided by day and night.

THE DAY IS YOURS, THE NIGHT ALSO IS YOURS; YOU HAVE PREPARED THE LIGHT AND THE SUN. YOU HAVE SET ALL THE BORDERS OF THE EARTH; YOU HAVE MADE SUMMER AND WINTER.

PSALM 74:16-17 NKJV

Not only are these opposites helpful to us in defining or "bordering" our lives, but they can also help us release stress.

Very often people who are engaged in physical, muscle-intensive work all day choose a mental activity with which to relax and unwind. Those who have idea-intensive jobs often enjoy relaxing with hobbies that make use of their hands, such as wood carving or needlework. Those in sterile, well-ordered environments look forward to coming home to weed their gardens.

Structured tasks and routines are good relaxation for those involved in the creative arts. The musician runs home to his computer. The surgeon delights in growing orchids in a hothouse. The factory worker enjoys crossword puzzles. The executive unwinds in the kitchen, preparing gourmet meals.

The Lord created us for this rhythm of opposites. God told Noah as he and his family left the ark that Noah would experience "seedtime and harvest, cold and heat, winter and summer, and day and night shall not cease" (Genesis 8:22 NKJV). Mankind was set in a world of opposites.

When you feel stressed out at day's end, try engaging in an activity that is opposite in nature to the work you have been doing. If you have been using your mind, turn to an activity that is physical. If you have been exerting physical energy, turn to an activity that is mental.

Let the pendulum swing back to rest in a central location!

PEOPLE WHO CANNOT FIND TIME FOR RECREATION ARE OBLIGED SOONER OR LATER TO FIND TIME FOR ILLNESS.

JOHN WANAMAKER

THE MIRACLE OF
A KIND WORD

The Reverend Purnell Bailey tells of a convict from Darlington, England, who had just been released from prison. He had spent three long years in prison for embezzlement, and though he wanted to return to his hometown, he was concerned about the social ostracism and possible ridicule he might have to endure from some of the townsfolk. Still, he was lonesome for his home and decided to risk the worst.

He had barely set foot on the main street of town when he encountered the mayor himself.

"Hello!" greeted the mayor in a cheery voice. "I'm glad to see you! How are you?" The man appeared ill at ease, so the mayor moved on.

Years later, the former mayor and the ex-convict accidentally met in another town. The latter said, "I want you to know what you did for me when I came out of prison."

"What did I do?" asked the mayor.

"You spoke a kind word to me and changed my life," replied the grateful man.[32]

We cannot always know how important the seed of a kind word may be to the one who receives it. More often than we know, words of encouragement or recognition provide a turning point in a person's outlook on life.

Just as Jesus spoke with love and acceptance to the hated tax collector Zaccheus, the mayor set the tone for others' contacts with the ex-convict by openly and warmly addressing him as a neighbor. People watch those they respect for cues regarding their own relationships with certain people.

Genuine, kind words cost the giver nothing but can mean the world to the one receiving them.

BE KIND: EVERYONE
YOU MEET IS FIGHTING
A HARD BATTLE.

IAN MACLAREN

YOU'RE ALL HEART

That twinge in your chest and that pain in your arm—is it just a muscle pull or is it something more serious, such as a heart problem? If it is your heart, what caused the problem, and what can you do to fix it?

When you consult your doctor, one of the first things he might ask is what kind of stress you are experiencing in your life. Most of us would answer, "Too much of the wrong kind." After all, it's not easy to cope with each day's major and minor irritations, people who annoy us, and events beyond our control.

> "COME TO ME,
> ALL YOU THAT
> ARE WEARY AND
> ARE CARRYING
> HEAVY BURDENS,
> AND I WILL GIVE
> YOU REST."
>
> MATTHEW 11:28 NRSV

In our world, stress is here to stay and many of us have heart problems (or loved ones who do). So how can we help ourselves?

Surgery and medication aren't always the answer. And, believe it or not, diet and exercise aren't necessarily the most important factors in restoring your heart's health. Studies have shown that having a spouse or other loved one to talk to and rely on, avoiding the traps of depression and anxiety, and having a sense that you can make a positive change in your condition can overcome the effects of even the most seriously blocked arteries.[33]

How often do we worry about things we can't do anything about? "Do not worry about tomorrow," Jesus said. "For tomorrow will worry about itself" (Matthew 6:34).

How often do we see ourselves as powerless? Remember what the Lord told Paul: "My grace is sufficient for you, for My strength is made perfect in weakness" (2 Corinthians 12:9 NKJV).

How often have we succumbed to depression and avoided contact with our spouses or friends? Paul told the early church, "Therefore encourage one another and build each other up" (1 Thessalonians 5:11).

We each have a part to play in our own physical and spiritual restoration and in the restoration of others. With God's help and the support of our brothers and sisters in the Lord, we can have healthy hearts.

AH, WHAT IS MORE BLESSED THAN
TO PUT OUR CARES AWAY.

GAIUS VALERIUS CATULLUS

BREWING GOOD RELATIONSHIPS

Most tea-drinkers would never consider tossing a tea bag in the nearest cup of hot water as the proper way to make a cup of tea. When one wants the best pot of tea, there are several rules for brewing that will assure the tea is a treat for the palate.

Always choose teas whose basic flavors are pleasing to you or your guests. If they are loose teas, don't be afraid to do a little blending, measuring one teaspoon per cup plus one teaspoon per pot. Let the tea steep for several minutes, but don't boil tea leaves. If you do, bitter tannins will emerge.

A WORD FITLY SPOKEN IS LIKE APPLES OF GOLD IN SETTINGS OF SILVER.

PROVERBS 25:11 NKJV

Like brewing tea, forming good relationships takes time and attention to be satisfying. Here are ten ways to show the love of Jesus to others—guaranteed to bring out the best "flavor" of each person:

1. Speak to people. There is nothing as nice as a cheerful word of greeting.

2. Smile at people. It takes 72 muscles to frown; 14 to smile.

3. Call people by name. The sweetest music is the sound of one's own name.

4. Be friendly and helpful.

5. Be cordial. Speak and act as if everything you do is a pleasure.

6. Be genuinely interested in people. You can like everybody if you try.

7. Be generous with praise—cautious with criticism.

8. Be considerate of the feelings of others. It will be appreciated.

9. Be thoughtful of the opinions of others.

10. Be alert to give service. What counts most in life is what we do for others.[34]

These things take time, but like the time spent perfecting that pot of tea, it is well worth the extra effort.

HOLD A TRUE FRIEND WITH
BOTH YOUR HANDS.

AFRICAN PROVERB

READ THE BOOK

Two women who were having lunch together in an elegant gourmet restaurant decided to end their repast with a cup of tea. The tea arrived and was poured into exquisite china teacups, but after taking the first sip, one woman complained to the waiter. "Sir, this tastes like benzene. Are you sure it's tea?"

The waiter replied, "Oh yes, it must be. The coffee tastes like turpentine."

If you are serving a pot of tea, you will have good results with this recipe:

1. Rinse out the teakettle and start with fresh, cold tap water. Never boil anything but water in your teakettle.

2. Bring the water to its first rolling boil. Never overboil! Overboiling takes the oxygen out of the water, which in turn creates a flat beverage.

3. Take the teapot to the teakettle and rinse out the pot with the boiling water from the kettle. Never take the kettle to the teapot, as you lose one

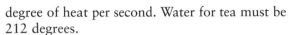
degree of heat per second. Water for tea must be 212 degrees.

4. Use one teabag or teaspoon of loose tea per cup. Leaves enter the warm teapot and the infusion begins when the leaf opens.

5. Pour hot water gently over the leaves. (Never bruise the leaves.)

6. Allow the tea to brew for three to five minutes, according to the blend of tea and how strong you like it.[35]

Following the instructions of connoisseurs can help us make a good cup of tea. The same is true of our spiritual lives, the Bible being God's instruction book: "All Scripture is given by inspiration of God, and is profitable for doctrine, for reproof, for correction, for instruction in righteousness" (2 Timothy 3:16 NKJV). We are wise to follow its instructions!

THE BIBLE IS GOD'S CHART FOR YOU TO STEER BY, TO KEEP YOU FROM THE BOTTOM OF THE SEA, AND TO SHOW YOU WHERE THE HARBOUR IS, AND HOW TO REACH IT WITHOUT RUNNING ON ROCKS AND BARS.

HENRY WARD BEECHER

EASY, ALBERT!

Even the well-controlled temper can find itself sorely tested on days when nothing seems to go according to plan. As the shadows lengthen, occasionally the fuse gets shorter.

One young father with a new baby discovered a secret to handling his temper. Desiring to take full part in the raising of his infant son, he cared for the baby on his days off, while his wife worked a part-time job. On one particular day, his son seemed to scream constantly. The father thought a visit to the park might distract the child.

> A WRATHFUL MAN STIRRETH UP STRIFE: BUT HE THAT IS SLOW TO ANGER APPEASETH STRIFE.
>
> PROVERBS 15:18 KJV

He pushed the child's stroller along at an easy pace and appeared to be unruffled by his still-crying baby. A mother with her baby strolled near them, and she heard him speaking softly, "Easy, Albert. Control yourself." The baby cried all the louder. "Now, now, Albert, keep your temper," he said.

Amazed at the father's calm, the mother said, "I must congratulate you on your self-control. You surely know how to speak to a baby—calmly and gently!" She patted the crying baby on the head and asked soothingly, "What's wrong, Albert?"

"No, no." explained the father, "The baby's name is Johnny. I'm Albert!"

Albert had stumbled onto something that actually works better with adults than with babies and children. When others lose their temper or seem to be baiting you intentionally, practice speaking in your most calm, quiet voice. In most cases, your tranquil demeanor will help the other person to calm down as it lengthens your own fuse.

Hard to do? Sure. But try this: Allow the other person to finish speaking his thoughts. Then, before you reply, take a deep breath. As you exhale think to yourself, *Jesus, I love You*. Keep it up every time you respond. The powerful name of Jesus can calm even the angriest seas of temper!

A MAN WHO CAN'T CONTROL
HIS TEMPER IS LIKE A CITY
WITHOUT DEFENSES.

JEWISH PROVERB

A Sip at a Time

The great movie maker Cecil B. DeMille once remarked on the importance of happiness in one's life and how to savor it:

> The profession one chooses to follow for a livelihood seldom brings fame and fortune, but a life lived within the dictates of one's conscience can bring happiness and satisfaction of living far beyond worldly acclaim. I expect to pass through this world but once, and any good therefore that I can do, or any kindness that I can show to any fellow creature, let me do it now. Let me not defer or neglect it, for I shall not pass this way again. Happiness must be sipped, not drained from life in great gulps—nor does it flow in a steady stream like water from a faucet. 'A portion of thyself' is a sip of happiness as satisfying as it is costless.[36]

MY SERVANTS
WILL SING OUT
OF THE JOY OF
THEIR HEARTS.

ISAIAH 65:14

One of the ways in which we may experience true happiness is to "sip" from the supply of talents and abilities God gives us and use them to benefit others. "Sipping" doesn't require spending great amounts of time. Neither does it require extraordinary or professional helping skills.

Use a gift or talent you have to serve others. Volunteer for a committee at work, teach Sunday school, join a choir or musical group, coach little league, teach adults to read, or simply make an effort to get better acquainted with your students.

Helen Keller, blind and deaf from the age of nineteen months, had remarkable sight when it came to viewing life's priorities. She said, "Many persons have a wrong idea about what constitutes true happiness. It is not attained through self-gratification, but through fidelity to a worthy purpose."

How miraculous it is that God has built an automatic measure of happiness into every act of self-sacrifice. Take a sip of happiness by serving others!

HE STANDS ERECT BY BENDING
OVER THE FALLEN. HE RISES
BY LIFTING OTHERS.

ROBERT GREEN INGERSOLL

COPING SKILLS

MY TIMES ARE IN YOUR HAND.

PSALM 31:15 NRSV

How we handle delays tells us a lot about ourselves. How do you handle a traffic jam when you left the house already late for work? What do you do when your flight is delayed because of mechanical difficulty or bad weather? How do you respond when the register in your checkout lane runs out of tape just as you get to the head of the line? Can you take a deep breath and enjoy a five-minute break at the railroad crossing when the guard rail goes down to allow a train to pass?

Consider how one man handled a delay. Just as the light turned green at the busy intersection, his car stalled in heavy traffic. He tried everything he knew to get the car started again, but all his efforts failed. The chorus of honking behind him put him on edge, which only made matters worse.

Finally he got out of his car and walked back to the first driver and said, "I'm sorry, but I can't seem to get my car started. If you'll go up there and give it a try, I'll stay here and blow your horn for you."

Things rarely go as smoothly as we would like, and we don't usually schedule ourselves any extra time "just in case" something goes wrong.

The ability to accept disappointments, delays, and setbacks with a pleasant, generous spirit is a gift of graciousness that comes from one who has received grace from others in pressured circumstances. Life is a series of choices, and no matter what situation we are in, we *always* have the freedom to choose how we are going to respond.

Refuse to get out of sorts the next time your schedule gets interrupted or turned upside down. Pray for strength to remain calm, cheerful, relaxed, and refreshed in the midst of the crisis. And always remember: God's plans for you are not thwarted by delays!

NEVER THINK THAT GOD'S
DELAYS ARE GOD'S DENIALS.
HOLD ON; HOLD FAST;
HOLD OUT. PATIENCE
IS GENIUS.

COMTE GEORGES-LOUIS LECLERC
DE BUFFON

MISSED MANNERS

During the Coolidge Administration, an overnight guest at the White House found himself in a terribly embarrassing predicament. At the family breakfast table, he was seated at the president's right hand. To his surprise he saw Coolidge take his coffee cup, pour the greater portion of its contents into the deep saucer, and leisurely add a little bit of cream and sugar.

BEFORE HONOUR IS HUMILITY.

PROVERBS 15:33 KJV

The guest was so disconcerted he lost his head. With a panicky feeling that it was incumbent upon him to do as the president did, he hastily poured his own coffee into his saucer. But he froze with horror as he watched Coolidge place his own saucer on the floor for the cat![37]

We may never have been guests at the White House, but we have all been in uncomfortable situations where we were unsure of ourselves and the proper etiquette for the occasion. Scripture describes the proper protocol for entering the presence of God. The psalmist tells us, "Enter into His gates with thanksgiving, and into His courts with praise" (Psalm 100:4 NKJV). We go into the Lord's presence with gratitude and joy for all He is and does in our lives.

King David asked, "Who may ascend into the hill of the LORD? Or who may stand in His holy place?" and then answered, "He who has clean hands and a pure heart, who has not lifted up his soul to an idol, nor sworn deceitfully" (Psalm 24:3-4 NKJV).

The writer of the Book of Hebrews said that Jesus made a way to God for us. We can approach His throne with confidence and "receive mercy and find grace to help us in our time of need" (Hebrews 4:16).

We don't have to worry about *how* we come to the Lord when we approach with pure and expectant hearts, understanding that before honor comes humility.

A MAN CAN COUNTERFEIT LOVE,
HE CAN COUNTERFEIT FAITH,
HE CAN COUNTERFEIT HOPE
AND ALL THE OTHER GRACES,
BUT IT IS VERY DIFFICULT
TO COUNTERFEIT HUMILITY.

DWIGHT LYMAN MOODY

AN OPEN DOOR

One warm summer afternoon, a woman was attending the baptism of her grandniece in a great old stone church in the English countryside. The massive doors of the church were flung wide to allow the warm sunshine into the chilly stone structure.

As she sat enjoying the ritual, a small bird flew in through the open doors. Full of fear, it flew backward and forward near the ceiling, vainly looking for a way out into the sunshine. Seeing the light coming through the dark stained glass windows, it flew to one, then the next, and finally back toward the ceiling. It continued flying about in this way for several minutes, quickly exhausting its strength in frenzied panic. The woman watched the bird with concern and frustration. How foolish he was not to fly back out the same door through which he had entered!

I RUN IN THE PATH OF YOUR COMMANDS, FOR YOU HAVE SET MY HEART FREE.

PSALM 119:32

Nearly ready to fall to the floor, the bird made a final lunge for one of the large rafters. Realizing he was in no immediate danger, he hopped a little on the beam, turned around, and suddenly saw the open door. Without hesitation he flew out into the sunshine, loudly singing a joyful song as he went.

The bird had captivated the woman's imagination. Suddenly she realized that she was like the bird. She had flitted about, trying to live a "good" life of noble works without recognizing that the door of salvation had been open to her all the time. She suddenly understood that to avoid flying errantly into places that offered no hope of eternal life, she need only stop flapping and be still in the Lord's presence. From that vantage point, she could better see the door of grace that He had prepared for her.

During your break today, let your spirit fly up to a high place and sit with the Lord. He will show you how to fly out of your current problems.

GOD GIVES THE SHOULDER
ACCORDING TO THE BURDEN.

GERMAN PROVERB

LIGHTENING UP

Are you a strict constructionist or a loose constructionist? These terms came into vogue after the U.S. Constitution was adopted. A strict constructionist takes the document exactly as it is; a loose constructionist sees room for different applications and interpretations.

When it comes to your daily schedule, are you strict or loose? Do you refuse to deviate from your to do list, or are you easygoing enough to shift gears when opportunity knocks at your door?

A young mother with four small children had given up on ever finding time for a break. Her husband frequently worked overtime, which meant she was totally responsible for taking care of the house and the children. She had decided the only way to make it all work was to be as rigid as a drill sergeant.

Certain chores had to be performed at a set time each day and on certain days of the week. If not, she felt pressured to make up for lost time by staying up later or getting up earlier—which drained her energy, made her cranky, and resulted in getting less done the following day.

One afternoon, her five-year-old daughter came into the kitchen, where she was planning dinner. "Come to my tea party," she said, a big smile on her face. Normally, Mom would have said, "Not now; I'm busy." But that day she had a flashback to her own five-year-old self inviting her mother to a tea party and being turned down.

Instead of saying no, she helped her daughter put together a tray containing a plate of cookies, some sandwiches cut into bite-size pieces, a small pot of tea, sugar and cream, her best teaspoons, and a couple of linen napkins. The two oldest children were at school. The youngest was napping. The house was quiet, and the young mother couldn't remember when she'd enjoyed a cup of tea so much.

ENJOY THE BLESSINGS OF THIS DAY, IF GOD SENDS THEM; AND THE EVILS OF IT BEAR PATIENTLY AND SWEETLY: FOR THIS DAY ONLY IS OURS, WE ARE DEAD TO YESTERDAY, AND WE ARE NOT YET BORN TO THE MORROW.

JEREMY TAYLOR

Power Naps

Medical students are usually adept at taking power naps. They fall asleep immediately upon lying down, sleep for fifteen to twenty minutes, and then awake refreshed. Researchers have discovered these short naps are actually more beneficial than longer midday naps. The body relaxes but does not fall into a "deep sleep," which can cause grogginess and disorientation.

WITH HIM IS AN ARM OF FLESH; BUT WITH US IS THE LORD OUR GOD TO HELP US, AND TO FIGHT OUR BATTLES. AND THE PEOPLE RESTED THEMSELVES UPON THE WORDS OF HEZEKIAH KING OF JUDAH.

2 CHRONICLES 32:8 KJV

Only one thing is required for people to fall asleep this quickly and benefit fully from a power nap—the ability to "turn off the mind." We quiet our minds by not thinking about all that remains to be done, worrying about all that might happen, or fretting over events in the past.

Power nappers are experts at inducing a form of inner peace that comes from knowing all will be well with the world while they check out for a few minutes. What they believe with their minds actually helps their bodies relax.

When King Hezekiah told the people that the Lord was with

them and would fight their battles, they *rested* upon his words. His words gave them inner peace, confidence, and a rest for their souls.

We can take those same words to heart today. The Lord is with us also, to help us and to fight our battles. These simple lyrics from a Bible-school chorus say it well:

YOU WORRY AND YOU WONDER HOW YOU'RE GONNA GET IT DONE, FROM THE RISING OF THE MOON 'TIL THE SETTING OF THE SUN. PLENTY TO DO WHEN YOUR REST IS THROUGH, LET HIM HAVE THE WORLD FOR A TURN OR TWO. THERE WILL BE PLENTY TO DO WHEN YOU WAKE UP . . . SO SLEEP ON FOR A FEW MINUTES. NOT WITHOUT DESIGN DOES GOD WRITE THE MUSIC OF OUR LIVES. BE IT OURS TO LEARN THE TIME, AND NOT BE DISCOURAGED AT THE RESTS. THEY ARE NOT TO BE SLURRED OVER, NOT TO BE OMITTED, NOT TO DESTROY THE MELODY, NOT TO CHANGE THE KEYNOTE. IF WE LOOK UP, GOD HIMSELF WILL BEAT THE TIME FOR US. WITH THE EYE ON HIM, WE SHALL STRIKE THE NEXT NOTE FULL AND CLEAR.

JOHN RUSKIN

THIRST-QUENCHERS

Water is essential to the survival of plants, animals, and people. The life processes of an organism depend on its cells having moisture. A tree, for example, may be 80 percent sap, which is primarily water. Sap contains minerals, carbohydrates, vitamins, and proteins, which circulate through the tree's vascular system to feed all parts of the tree.

The amount of the water supply in an area determines whether it is a desert or a forest. It determines whether a tree is shriveled and stunted or towering and majestic. Water comes to trees through dew, clouds, mists, fog, summer rains, and winter snows. Trees also take in water through their roots, which tap into springs, streams, or rivers.

A tree does not hoard moisture for itself, but after the water travels through the framework of the tree, it is given off into the surrounding air. The moisture, along with the oxygen expelled into the air, gives the forest a fresh fragrance.

WHOSOEVER WILL, LET HIM TAKE THE WATER OF LIFE FREELY.

REVELATION 22:17 KJV

The spiritual lesson we learn from nature is that it is nearly impossible to be a blessing to others when we are grossly undernourished ourselves. Like the tree, we must be well watered with God's Word and His Spirit to bring a sweet fragrance to those around us.

If you are feeling empty and dry today, go to the watering hole of God's Word and take a long, refreshing drink. Feel His truth permeate every cell of your being and rejuvenate love, peace, and joy in your heart. It won't be long until you're looking for ways to help someone else!

TAKE REST; A FIELD THAT HAS
RESTED GIVES A BOUNTIFUL CROP.

OVID

FIRE!

BE PLEASED, O LORD, TO DELIVER ME:
O LORD, MAKE HASTE TO HELP ME.

Psalm 40:13 kjv

It's usually a couple of hours before the final bell rings when we realize that the clock's been moving faster than we have. So we break into a mental sprint to see if we can beat the clock to the day's finish line.

It's usually about this time of day when everyone and everything needs immediate attention. Sometimes we end the day thinking all we did for the last few hours was "put out brush fires." Consequently, the primary objectives of the day stand waiting for attention.

With the usual candor of children, one kindergartner shed some light on this afternoon dilemma. He was on a class field trip to the fire station to take a tour and learn about fire safety.

The fireman explained what to do in case of a fire. "First, go to the door and feel it to see if it's hot. Then, if you smell or see smoke coming in around the door, fall to your knees. Does anyone know why you ought to fall to your knees?"

The little boy piped up and said, "Sure! To start praying to ask God to get us out of this mess!"

What a good idea for those brush fires that break out in the heat the day! If we mentally and spiritually fall to our knees, we move our thoughts to God's presence around us and His authority over the circumstances we are facing.

Falling to our knees puts us beneath the "smoke" of confusion and enables us to breathe in gulps of reason, calm, and clarity. We are in a better position to see a way out of the burning room and move in an efficient and productive direction.

By giving us knees on which to fall, God has already answered our prayer for help. Bowing down for prayer reminds us who has ultimate control over the situation and puts us in communication with Him. He allows us to see how to rescue the day from the crunch time.

Sometimes your quiet time becomes a "falling on your knees" time!

A MAN PRAYED, AND AT
FIRST HE THOUGHT THAT
PRAYER WAS TALKING. BUT
HE BECAME MORE AND
MORE QUIET UNTIL IN THE
END HE REALIZED THAT
PRAYER IS LISTENING.

SØREN AABYE KIERKEGAARD

NIGHT GLORIES

Some of the most fragrant flowers in the garden stay tightly closed, or "sleep," during the day. They open only later in the afternoon and evening, perfuming the night air with their sweet scents.

The most magnificent of these late-bloomers is the moonflower. Moonflowers look like white morning glories, except that their blossoms are enormous—up to eight inches across. Each bloom lasts for only one night, but the scent more than makes up for the short performance.[38]

Just as nature lends itself to day and night creations, so there are "morning people" who feel their best in the early hours of the day and "night people" who seem to bloom after dark. If you are a late bloomer, fill the night air with the sweet fragrance of prayer before God this evening.

> LET MY PRAYER BE SET FORTH BEFORE THEE AS INCENSE; AND THE LIFTING UP OF MY HANDS AS THE EVENING SACRIFICE.
>
> PSALM 141:2 KJV

The Lord looks forward to your companionship and is waiting to hear from you. Give Him your attention and listen to what He wants to tell you. Treat God as you would a dear friend.

Review your schedule to find time you can commit to God. Have no time? You may be overlooking some ready-made times, such as your drive to and from work. Find a place of isolation without distractions.

Jesus said, "Enter your closet" (Matthew 6:6 KJV). This "closet" can be any place, any time you can be alone with Him. Or you may want to designate one special place where you pray.

As you spend time seeking God during the night, you will bring a sweet fragrance into the throne room of God. The Bible describes this beautifully in Revelation 8:3 KJV: Another angel came and stood at the altar, having a golden censer; and there was given unto him much incense, that he should offer it with the prayers of all saints upon the golden altar which was before the throne.

Enjoy your night glories.

ALL THE CHRISTIAN VIRTUES ARE
LOCKED UP IN THE WORD PRAYER.

CHARLES HADDON SPURGEON

WORRY WEDNESDAY

Many people lose sleep by worrying. They lie awake in bed, wondering if they made a right decision the day before—if they did the wrong thing—and what they should do tomorrow.

Here's a creative way one woman handled worry. With so many things to worry about, she decided to set aside one day each week to worry. As worrying situations occurred, she wrote them down and put them in her worry box. Then, on Worry Wednesday, she read through each worry. To her amazement, most of the things she had been disturbed about had already been taken care of in some way. Thus, she learned there was seldom a justifiable reason to worry. As the psalmist wrote in Psalm 127:2 NKJV, It is vain for you to rise up early, to sit up late, to eat the bread of sorrows; for so He gives His beloved sleep.

American poet Ellen M. Huntington Gates described God's perfect rest for those with weary hearts in her poem "Sleep Sweet."

> Sleep sweet within this
>   quiet room,
> O thou, whoe'er thou art,

"DO NOT WORRY ABOUT TOMORROW, FOR TOMORROW WILL WORRY ABOUT ITS OWN THINGS. SUFFICIENT FOR THE DAY IS ITS OWN TROUBLE."

MATTHEW 6:34 NKJV

And let no mournful yesterdays
Disturb thy peaceful heart.
Nor let tomorrow mar thy rest
With dreams of coming ill:
Thy Maker is thy changeless friend,
His love surrounds thee still.
Forget thyself and all the world,
Put out each garish light:
The stars are shining overhead
Sleep sweet! Good night! Good night![39]

As a child of God, you can rest in the knowledge that you are surrounded by a loving Father who cares for you. Jesus said, "Look at the birds of the air, for they neither sow nor reap nor gather into barns; yet your heavenly Father feeds them. Are you not of more value than they?" (Matthew 6:26 NKJV). The same Creator who placed each star in the sky is watching over you.

THE BEGINNING OF ANXIETY
IS THE END OF FAITH; AND
THE BEGINNING OF TRUE
FAITH IS THE END OF ANXIETY.

GEORGE MULLER

An Angel in Deed

DO NOT FORGET TO ENTERTAIN
STRANGERS, FOR BY SO DOING
SOME PEOPLE HAVE ENTERTAINED
ANGELS WITHOUT KNOWING IT.

HEBREWS 13:2

The hospital room was quiet. Natalie, who was new to the area, was facing an emergency operation the next morning. Knowing only a few people in this small town added to her anxiety. She was alone in the hospital room, and the quietness of the room closed in on her.

She was ready to cry when she heard the creaking of the door. She looked toward it and saw a kind young face.

"Hi," the young woman said. "Are you lonely?"

"I sure am," Natalie replied.

"I'm a nursing student and have been observing here for a couple of weeks. I've caught up on all my paperwork. Do you feel like talking?" she asked.

"I sure do," Natalie replied gratefully. She straightened her pillow and slowly propped herself up in bed.

The compassion in the student's eyes comforted Natalie as their conversation soon turned to God and His wonderful and amazing grace. During the conversation, the heavy burden of fear in Natalie's heart began to lift. After a couple of hours, she finally drifted off to sleep. The young woman quietly left the room.

Natalie never saw the student nurse again. She couldn't even remember her name. But she never forgot the comfort and peace that settled over her as the young woman shared her love for Jesus Christ. The next morning, Natalie asked about the student nurse, but no one on the new shift had a clue as to her identity.

Whether the young woman was a celestial angel or an earthly angel of mercy, she was an angel in deed. She brought peace to Natalie's heart and joy to her soul. Isn't that precisely what God sends His angels to do?

AROUND OUR PILLOWS
GOLDEN LADDERS RISE,
AND UP AND DOWN THE
SKIES, WITH WINGED
SANDALS SHOD, THE ANGELS
COME AND GO, THE
MESSENGERS OF GOD!

RICHARD HENRY STODDARD

YESTERDAY'S DIAPERS

Patricia had a habit of ignoring others whenever she was particularly busy. One evening her husband complained, "I feel like yesterday's diapers." Patricia told him that she was simply busy and didn't mean to treat him badly, but as she fell asleep that night she thought about what he had said. Had she been ignoring him?

She thought about her busy days filled with teaching school, changing diapers, grocery shopping, laundry, school plays, parent-teacher meetings, and volunteer work. She felt exhausted just thinking about it. Brushing off her husband's concerns, she dropped into a deep sleep.

THESE THINGS I
COMMAND YOU,
THAT YE LOVE
ONE ANOTHER.

JOHN 15:17 KJV

Then one day she discovered for herself just how he felt. She had dropped by the offices of a well-known organization to leave some information. She had hoped to meet and talk with some of the volunteers, but to Patricia's surprise everyone was too busy to speak with her. Convinced that she was not welcome, she left in discouragement.

In our busy world, we often ignore one another. Many of us are overworked and overextended, and we find that it's easy to make a habit of ignoring others, including those we love the most. But we can make a difference in the lives of the people around us by taking the time to listen to them—by showing them that they are precious to God and to us.

Jesus Christ said that the greatest commandment of all is to love one another and that His followers would be known by their love—a deep and abiding love. So today, as you go about your day, take a moment from your busyness. Make a call and tell a friend that you think she's special. Not only will you brighten up your friend's day, you'll also speak volumes to a hurting and neglected world.

FAITH, LIKE LIGHT, SHOULD ALWAYS BE SIMPLE AND UNBENDING; WHILE LOVE, LIKE WARMTH, SHOULD BEAM FORTH ON EVERY SIDE AND BEND TO EVERY NECESSITY OF OUR BRETHREN.

MARTIN LUTHER

IN THE DARK

Did you ever go exploring through the woods as a child? Following an unfamiliar path seems like an adventure until it gets dark. While hiking up a mountainous trail, you lose track of time, and murky shadows creep in. The sound of twigs and leaves cracking under your shoes grows deafening. Your great adventure now turns frightening. Suddenly, you can't see the path in front of you. If only another person would come along with a lantern and lead you back home.

Today, there are many people who walk in darkness. They are confused about their purpose in life and are searching for answers. They need someone to hold out a light and show them the way.

Psalm 18:28 NKJV says, "For You will light my lamp; the LORD my God will enlighten my darkness."

In our spiritual darkness of hopelessness and lack of direction, God promises to bring hope to our situation with His brilliant light of wisdom and understanding. Often that wisdom comes through the words of people we know or strangers we meet. Have you walked down a difficult road? Then share what God taught you in that situation. Lead others out of the darkness into a life filled with meaning and purpose. Share God's light with someone who is searching for the truth.

CHRIST HAS TURNED ALL
OUR SUNSETS INTO DAWNS.

CLEMENT OF ALEXANDRIA

A CHILD'S WORDS

> "TRULY I TELL YOU, WHOEVER DOES NOT
> RECEIVE THE KINGDOM OF GOD AS
> A LITTLE CHILD WILL NEVER ENTER IT."
>
> MARK 10:15 NRSV

Anne was visiting her mother one late winter day when the temperature, which had given a hint of spring that morning, took a drop back to freezing. Anne had left home that morning with only a sweater to keep her warm. Since she had other things to do before going home, she asked to borrow one of her mother's jackets.

Later in the afternoon, Anne went by the day-care center to pick up her son, Jacob, a typical four-year-old who usually gives his mother a full-blown account of how his day went with the other children as soon she picks him up. This time he noticed that she was wearing the same kind of jacket that he was wearing, and he asked where she got her new denim jacket. She told him that she borrowed it from his grandmother. Jacob reached down and lifted the sleeve to his nose.

"Oh, Mom!" he said. "It smells!" She asked him what he meant. Did the jacket smell bad?

Jacob replied, "No, Mommy. It smells good—just like Grandma does!"

The next day Anne told her mother what Jacob had said, little realizing the impact her words had. To have a child identify you by smell evokes a personal and precious feeling; Jacob's comments made his grandmother feel loved in a special way.

Children accept us as we are, without any pretense. They expect us to be who we are and not the image we present to the world. That's the way God wants us to appear before Him. He already knows what we're going to say before we say it.

Today, be as direct as a child and tell Him precisely what you need and want. God will hear you and respond in His time and in His way. He always answers your prayers.

ANYTHING LARGE ENOUGH
FOR A WISH TO LIGHT
UPON IS LARGE ENOUGH
TO HANG A PRAYER ON.

GEORGE MACDONALD

THE BUTTERFLY INSIDE

Jean Thompson stood in front of her fifth-grade class on the first day of school and told them that she loved each child in the class equally. But she knew that wasn't entirely true, because there in front of her was a little boy named Teddy Stoddard.

Mrs. Thompson had watched Teddy the year before and noticed he didn't play well with the other children. His clothes were unkempt, and he always seemed to need a bath.

When Mrs. Thompson reviewed Teddy's records, she found that his first-grade teacher had written, "Teddy is a bright, inquisitive child." His second-grade teacher wrote, "Teddy is well liked by his classmates, but troubled because his mother has a terminal illness." His third-grade teacher wrote, "Teddy continues to work hard, but his mother's death has affected him." Teddy's fourth-grade teacher wrote, "Teddy is withdrawn. . . ."

At Christmas, Teddy brought Mrs. Thompson a present. She opened the package and found a rhinestone bracelet with some of the stones missing and a partial bottle of cologne. She mentioned how pretty the bracelet was and dabbed some of the perfume behind her wrist. Teddy said, "Mrs. Thompson, today you smell just like my mom used to."[40]

Just as Mrs. Thompson realized that she had let Teddy's physical appearance and poor attitude color her judgment of him, many of us are guilty of doing the same thing at times. The words and actions of other people can wound a tender spirit, especially that of a child.

As you reflect upon your day, ask yourself how your actions impacted other people? It's important to remember that Jesus loved everyone regardless of position in life, character, intelligence, or physical beauty. The Bible says, "Love thy neighbor." It doesn't say love them only if they're pretty, or the mayor, or the minister. Remember, there is nothing in a caterpillar that tells you it's going to be a butterfly.

DO NOT JUDGE MEN BY MERE
APPEARANCES; FOR THE LIGHT
LAUGHTER THAT BUBBLES ON THE LIP
OFTEN MANTLES OVER THE DEPTHS
OF SADNESS, AND THE SERIOUS
LOOK MAY BE THE SOBER VEIL THAT
COVERS A DIVINE PEACE AND JOY.

EDWIN HUBBELL

SAVOR THE MOMENT

Ann described a lesson she learned after the painful loss of her sister. Her brother-in-law opened the bottom drawer of her sister's bureau and lifted out a tissue-wrapped package. "This," he said, "is not a slip. This is lingerie." He discarded the tissue and handed the slip to Ann. It was exquisite silk, handmade and trimmed with a cobweb of lace. The price tag, bearing an astronomical figure, was still attached.

"Jan bought this the first time we went to New York nine years ago. She never wore it. She was saving it for a special occasion. Well, I guess this is the occasion." He took the slip from Ann and put it on the bed with the other clothes they planned to take to the funeral home. His hands lingered on the soft material for a moment, then he slammed the drawer shut and turned to Ann. "Don't ever save anything for a special occasion. Every day you're alive is a special occasion."

She remembered those words throughout the funeral and the days that followed. Ann thought about all the things that her sister had done without realizing they

TEACH US TO NUMBER OUR DAYS, THAT WE MAY APPLY OUR HEARTS UNTO WISDOM.

PSALM 90:12 KJV

were special. The words her brother-in-law spoke changed her life.

Ann now spends more time with her family and friends and less time in committee meetings. Now she enjoys the view from her deck without fussing about the weeds in the garden. She's not saving anything either; her family uses the good china and crystal for every special event—such as losing a pound, unclogging the sink, or spying the first camellia blossom of the season.

As you watch the breathless beauty of a sunset or the colorful splendor of a rainbow, savor the moment. Cherish the brilliance of the maple leaf nipped by frost and the white clouds floating across the crystal blue sky. Remember that every moment of every day is special.

SO HERE HATH BEEN DAWNING
ANOTHER BLUE DAY; THINK, WILT
THOU LET IT SLIP USELESS AWAY?

THOMAS CARLYLE

A SPECIAL MISSION

> "WHOEVER WELCOMES A
> LITTLE CHILD LIKE THIS IN
> MY NAME WELCOMES ME."
>
> MATTHEW 18:5

Sam's wife hadn't attended a worship service for more than thirty years. Sunday after Sunday, the elderly deacon walked in and found his seat alone on the second pew. Newcomers thought he was single, but the established members knew the truth. He was a dedicated soul who lived his life serving and praising His Father in Heaven. He passed out candy to the little ones and expressed his love freely among the members of the quaint church.

Although his wife, Helen, wasn't present during the worship service, she was there in spirit with her husband. She also supported the pastor with her prayers and fattened him up with her delightful chocolate desserts. Over the chatter of little mouths and the screaming of infants, she faithfully listened to his sermons by intercom.

Sam and Helen were always the first ones to arrive for every service. Helen had an important job to do and took it quite seriously. As director of the church nursery, she wanted to be early and ready before the little ones arrived. Each and every day of the week, she lifted her babies up in prayer before she retired for the night. She loved each special one as if it were her own.

Many women offered to relieve her, but she wouldn't allow it. God had called her to this service, and it was her intention to continue with it as long as possible. Over the years, "her" babies grew to adulthood and presented her with children of their own. She was truly loved by all.

As she rocked and sang to each child, she was serving her God in a powerful way. She provided a safe and warm environment for the little ones, while their parents fed on the Word of God.

God has a job for each of us. This woman found hers in the care of tiny babies. Tonight, ask God how you can serve Him best.

A CANDLE LOSES
NOTHING BY LIGHTING
ANOTHER CANDLE.

AUTHOR UNKNOWN

GOD'S TREASURES

Up on the hillside in a quiet community stands a quaint little country church. Its steeple stands proud, and its stained-glass windows provide a welcoming atmosphere to everyone who passes by. As the wind blows, the tall trees bow down over the church as if they are protecting the outside walls of the magnificent but small structure.

"COME TO ME,
ALL YOU WHO
ARE WEARY AND
BURDENED,
AND I WILL
GIVE YOU REST."

MATTHEW 11:28

On Wednesday nights and Sunday mornings, the church comes alive with enthusiasm and laughter, as its dedicated members come to worship God. During that time, love is evident as friends and family members embrace each other with warm hugs and handshakes.

During the week, the church is normally quiet. Periodically, someone will stop by to walk around the yard, while admiring the beauty it bestows. This place is truly God's house, a holy and sanctified building. Many times a passerby will slow his pace and see the beauty it holds, but sadly too many people speed by without even acknowledging its existence.

Unfortunately, these people regard God in the same manner as they do His church building. Their days are too busy. They speed through life without seeking His Will for their lives or enjoying His everlasting love for them. As God looks upon the earth, He probably sheds a tear knowing that some of His children are simply surviving life rather than living an abundant life. He offers a life full of hope and peace.

God will not force a person to stop to smell the roses, to ponder the history of His house, or to worship Him. But when a passerby glances toward the church and lifts a few words to Him, He rejoices with the angels in Heaven. Like salvation, the opportunity to stop, to rest in His hands, and enjoy the treasures that God gives is available to all who will take the time to accept His gift.

> YOU WAKE UP IN THE MORNING WITH TWENTY-FOUR HOURS OF THE UNMANUFACTURED TISSUE OF THE UNIVERSE OF YOUR LIFE. IT IS YOURS. IT IS THE MOST PRECIOUS OF POSSESSIONS. NO ONE CAN TAKE IT FROM YOU. IT IS UNSTEALABLE. AND NO ONE RECEIVES EITHER MORE OR LESS.
>
> ARNOLD BENNETT

WHO'S IN CONTROL?

Wendy jumped at the opportunity—two full weeks alone to write. Looking forward to her "writer's retreat," she eagerly packed her car with everything she would need and drove away from her house. Finally she reached her destination—a cabin on a deserted road, almost hidden by overgrown bushes.

That first evening, Wendy watched the sun dip behind the hardwood forest, leaving in its wake blackness so dense that, without moonlight, she couldn't see her hand in front of her face. Inside the cabin she refused to think about being alone in the middle of the woods and calmly stacked her writing books, dictionary, and paper next to the computer she had brought along.

Later, she worked on a poem, then stretched out on the loveseat. Picking up a novel, she began to read. As she yawned sleepily, the words on the page blurred, and she dozed off. Some time later, a noise in the attic awakened her. She bolted upright, her heart pounding in her ears. *Lord,* she thought, *please take this fear from me.*

"PEACE I LEAVE WITH YOU; MY PEACE I GIVE YOU. I DO NOT GIVE TO YOU AS THE WORLD GIVES. DO NOT LET YOUR HEARTS BE TROUBLED AND DO NOT BE AFRAID."

JOHN 14:27

Her breathing quickened as she walked silently to the bottom of the stairs and looked up at the locked attic. Easing up each narrow step, she felt a lump in her throat. Listening at the attic door, she realized to her great relief that the sound was merely mice scurrying across the wooden floor.

The next morning, Wendy thanked God for His ever-present help in time of trouble. Holding a mug of coffee, she walked down a pathway to the woods. Sun-dappled wildflowers greeted her, and lizards raced under rhododendron bushes. Around the next turn was a hidden waterfall. She sat down on a boulder and prayed, turning all her fears over to God, trusting Him to take care of her. During the rest of her stay at the cabin, her writing flowed as easily as the rush of water over river rocks.

TONIGHT, IF YOU NEED PEACE,
SEEK GOD'S. DROP THY STILL
DEWS OF QUIETNESS, TILL ALL
OUR STRIVINGS CEASE; TAKE FROM
OUR SOULS THE STRAIN AND STRESS,
AND LET OUR ORDERED LIVES
CONFESS THE BEAUTY OF THY PEACE.

JOHN GREENLEAF WHITTIER

HAVE YOU FORGIVEN?

> "IF YOU DO NOT FORGIVE MEN
> THEIR SINS, YOUR FATHER WILL
> NOT FORGIVE YOUR SINS."
>
> MATTHEW 6:15

One day Corrie ten Boom visited a friend in the hospital. Though her friend was quite ill, Corrie noticed that she also was quite bitter.

At first, the two women spent time catching up on each other's lives. Finally the woman said that her husband disliked having a sick wife, and as a result, he had left and was living with a younger woman. Knowing that her friend was greatly distressed, Corrie asked, "Have you forgiven him?"

The woman said, "Certainly not!"

Corrie remembered a time when she herself had been unforgiving. After World War II, she had recognized a nurse who had been cruel to her dying sister while they were detained in the Ravensbruck concentration camp. The memories flooded back, and she recalled how her sister had suffered because of this nurse.

She knew she must forgive, but she couldn't seem to bring herself to do it. She finally had a talk with God.

"Lord," she said, "You know I cannot forgive her. My sister suffered too much because of her cruelties." The Lord revealed Romans 5:5 KJV to Corrie: "The love of God is shed abroad in our hearts by the Holy Spirit which is given unto us." Then she prayed, "Thank You, Father, that Your love in me is stronger than my bitterness."

When she finally met the nurse, Corrie told her that although she had been bitter about what happened to her sister, now she loved her. By the end of their conversation, Corrie shared the way to salvation, and the nurse accepted Jesus Christ as her Lord and Savior.[41]

Forgiving someone else is powerful. It is a blessing to the one forgiven, but it also releases the one forgiving from the bondage of bitterness. If you need to forgive someone today, ask God to show you how.

FORGIVENESS IS MAN'S DEEPEST NEED AND HIGHEST ACHIEVEMENT.

HORACE BUSHNELL

IN JESUS' NAME

Thirty-seven-year-old Joyce Girgenti, a Christian artist, shares her faith by painting the name of Jesus into her inspirational paintings.

One year, Joyce was approached by an organization who wanted her to donate a Christmas card scene. Her first effort, a fireplace scene complete with a Christmas tree and nativity, was turned down. Undaunted, Joyce replaced the scene with another, and it was accepted. Later, Joyce realized why her original scene had been rejected—God had other plans.

Joyce had used a photo of her own fireplace to paint the original scene. Working from the top of the canvas, she painted the Christmas tree, the nativity on the mantel, the roaring fire, and the stones that formed the fireplace. As she began to paint the bottom of the fireplace, she turned to her daughter. "Wouldn't it be neat to hide something in the fireplace that refers to Christmas?" she asked.

Before her daughter could answer, Joyce said, "What better than Jesus? He's why we celebrate Christmas."

After her card was rejected, Joyce used it to send to clients and friends. One day, Joyce received a call from her friend Mary who asked, "Is Jesus' name really in your fireplace?" She had called to verify what she'd found.

Now, in each of her inspirational paintings, Joyce seeks to please God by painting Jesus' name somewhere in her work. She shares her faith with everyone she meets, saying, "If you forget me, you've lost nothing, but if you forget Jesus, you've lost everything."

It's a mystery trying to find His name so well hidden in Joyce's paintings, but the real mystery is not His name—it's Jesus himself. Only when Jesus is revealed are we able to discern His hidden treasure for us—His gift of salvation.

SIN SEPARATES, PAIN ISOLATES, BUT SALVATION AND COMFORT UNITE.

JULIAN OF NORWICH

BRINGING THE
SUNSHINE BACK

It was one of those wet rainy days at the end of winter, in that interlude between the cold weather and the warmth of spring, a time of daffodils peeking their bright yellow blossoms through the ground and offering promise of more to come.

In a small house on the corner, Rhonda, a young mother of three, was fixing lunch for her children. Their favorite sandwich was peanut butter and jelly. She brought the bread and peanut butter out of the cabinet and removed the blackberry jelly from the refrigerator. The lid on the jar of peanut butter seemed to be stuck tight. She tried and tried to open it, but the lid wouldn't budge.

> THE LORD GIVES STRENGTH TO HIS PEOPLE; THE LORD BLESSES HIS PEOPLE WITH PEACE.
>
> PSALM 29:11

Suddenly, Rhonda burst into tears. She had reached her limit. The baby had cried all night with colic, so she had gotten little rest; the two-year-old was his usual "terrible twos" self; the rain meant the kids couldn't play outside; and now the dumb lid to the peanut butter jar wouldn't come off.

At about that time, her five-year-old daughter came into the kitchen. Kylie had been playing with dolls in her bedroom when she heard her mother crying. The little girl hugged her mother around her waist and said, "Don't cry, Mommy. God will bring the sunshine back tomorrow."

Kylie's words put everything back into perspective for Rhonda. She knew that she had overreacted because she was so tired. Kylie was right. Tomorrow would be another day.

Most of us can probably put ourselves in this young mother's place. We've all felt we were at the end of our rope at some time or other. Sometimes the smallest incident causes us to spill over, making us believe we can't cope anymore. Whatever the situation, always remember that God—in the words of a small child—will bring the sunshine back tomorrow.

FOR MOST MEN THE WORLD IS
CENTERED IN SELF, WHICH IS
MISERY: TO HAVE ONE'S WORLD
CENTERED IN GOD IS PEACE.

DONALD HANKEY

ENCUMBRANCES

In Jules Verne's novel, *The Mysterious Island,* he tells of five men who escape a Civil War prison camp by hijacking a hot-air balloon. As they rise into the air, they realize the wind is carrying them over the ocean. Watching their homeland disappear on the horizon, they wonder how much longer the balloon will stay aloft.

As the hours pass and the surface of the ocean draws closer, the men decide they must cast some of the weight overboard, because they have no way to heat the air in the balloon. Shoes, overcoats, and weapons are reluctantly discarded, and the uncomfortable aviators feel their balloon rise.

However, it isn't long before they find themselves dangerously close to the waves again, so they toss their food overboard. Unfortunately, this, too, is only a temporary solution, and the craft again threatens to lower the men into the sea. One man has an idea: they can tie the ropes that hold the passenger car and sit on the ropes. Then they can cut away the basket beneath them. As they do this, the balloon rises again.

Not a minute too soon, they spot land. The five jump into the water and swim to the island. They are alive because they were able to discern the difference between what was really needed and what was not. The "necessities" they once thought they couldn't live without were the very weights that almost cost them their lives.

Why not make an honest assessment of the things that might be slowing you down today? Are they physical or spiritual necessities for you or someone you love? What would your life be like without them? If you eliminated them, would you have more time for the things in your life that really matter?

Ask God to show you how your life could be improved if you made some changes and dropped some things that are weighing you down.

I HAVE READ IN PLATO AND CICERO SAYINGS THAT ARE VERY WISE AND VERY BEAUTIFUL; BUT I NEVER READ IN EITHER OF THEM: "COME UNTO ME ALL YE THAT LABOUR AND ARE HEAVY LADEN."

SAINT AUGUSTINE OF HIPPO

THE IMPORTANCE OF EVERYDAY TALK

The banquet hall is festively adorned with beautiful flowers and ribbons. Across the front of the room, a large banner reads, "A Golden Congratulations for a Golden Couple." It is their fiftieth wedding anniversary, and family and friends have gathered from far and near to pay tribute to them. The four children each take a turn at describing their fondest memories and greatest lessons learned from their parents. Then the cake is cut, pictures are taken, and everyone enjoys visiting with one another.

Too soon, the afternoon draws to a conclusion. Friends say good-bye; family members repack mementos in the cars; and everyone leaves. Later that evening, one of the grandchildren asks, "What is the secret, Grandma, to being happily married for fifty years?" Without hesitation, her grandmother replies, "We have always been able to talk about everything."

Recent research supports her conclusion. A study of couples happily married for more than twenty-five years found only one thing they all had in common—each couple "chit-chatted" with each other daily. Perhaps, since they already know how to converse with one another, they are more able to talk out their differences when tough times come.

The same most likely holds true for our relationship with God. If we commune with Him regularly, then we will automatically turn to Him first when crisis comes.

Have you had a quiet time talking with God today?

I AM SORRY FOR MEN WHO DO NOT READ THE BIBLE EVERY DAY. I WONDER WHY THEY DEPRIVE THEMSELVES OF THE STRENGTH AND THE PLEASURE.

WOODROW WILSON

A PERMANENT COMPANION

What little girl wouldn't love to have a new doll? One that eats, wets, talks, walks—or one that is nothing but a silent bedtime companion. Every year the toy shelves burst with new models just waiting to be dubbed the child's favorite doll.

Author Dale Galloway shares a story by R. E. Thomas that makes us rethink just what constitutes a "favorite" among some children:

"Do you like dollies?" the little girl asked her house guest.

"Yes, very much," the man responded.

"Then I'll show you mine," was the reply. Thereupon she presented one by one of a whole family of dolls.

"And now tell me," the visitor asked, "which is your favorite doll?"

The child hesitated for a moment and then she said, "You're quite sure you like dollies? Will you please promise not to smile if I show you my favorite?" The man solemnly promised, and the girl hurried from the room. In a

> "SURELY I AM WITH YOU ALWAYS, TO THE VERY END OF THE AGE."
>
> MATTHEW 28:20

moment she returned with a tattered and dilapidated old doll. Its hair had come off; its nose was broken; its cheeks were scratched; an arm and leg were missing.

"Well, well," said the visitor, "and why do you like this one best?"

"I love her most," said the little girl, "because if I didn't love her, no one else would."[42]

God knows our condition: tattered lives, broken hearts, blind eyes, missing parts. If He didn't love us, no one else would. That's why He sent Jesus as a permanent companion for us—anytime, day or night.

GOD IS IN ALL THINGS AND IN EVERY PLACE. THERE IS NOT A PLACE IN THE WORLD IN WHICH HE IS NOT MOST TRULY PRESENT. JUST AS BIRDS, WHEREVER THEY FLY, ALWAYS MEET WITH THE AIR, SO WE, WHEREVER WE GO, OR WHEREVER WE ARE, ALWAYS FIND GOD PRESENT.

SAINT FRANCIS OF SALES

FESTIVAL OF LIGHTS

"LET YOUR LIGHT SHINE BEFORE MEN
IN SUCH A WAY THAT THEY MAY SEE
YOUR GOOD WORKS, AND GLORIFY
YOUR FATHER WHO IS IN HEAVEN."

MATTHEW 5:16 NASB

The menorah, a candelabra with four candles on each side and one in the middle, actually represents a miracle. It is used during the winter Jewish holiday known as Hanukkah or the Festival of Lights.

Hanukkah, which means *dedication*, commemorates the revolt against the Syrian Greeks in 167-164 B.C., when the Jews recaptured the temple and rededicated it to God's service.

The Greeks had extinguished the great seven-branched candelabra in the temple, and only enough oil remained for the light to burn one day. It took eight days for the priests to consecrate more oil. Nevertheless, the Jews lit the lampstand, and it continued to burn for eight full days!

Thus the Feast of Dedication, also called the Festival of Lights, was established. In Jewish homes the miniature menorah candles are lit, one each day, to represent the eight days. The center candle is the *shamash,* a Hebrew word meaning *servant,* and it is used to light the other candles. From Scripture, Christians know that Jesus is the Light of the World, God's *shamash.*[43]

The Jerusalem temple has been destroyed, but when we receive Christ, we become the temple of God, and the *shamash* shines in our hearts. We become lights in a dark world. Through His Holy Spirit, we have a never-ending supply of oil to keep our lamps brightly burning.

LIGHT IS ABOVE US, AND
COLOR AROUND US; BUT
IF WE HAVE NOT LIGHT
AND COLOR IN OUR EYES,
WE SHALL NOT PERCEIVE
THEM OUTSIDE US.

JOHANN WOLFGANG VON GOETHE

HEARING WITH
THE HEART

"We've wasted my whole Saturday," moaned John as his father gently woke him.

The plaintive, anguished tone of his voice created an instant reaction in his father and a flash of anger surged upward. It had been a very long day of painting and hanging wallpaper in Mom's new office, and Dad was tired. John had worked hard earlier in the day, but as the novelty wore off he became bored and eventually fell asleep on a couch in an adjacent office. Now his dad, Richard, was waking him so that they could head home.

BECAUSE THINE
HEART WAS
TENDER.

2 KINGS 22:19 KJV

Before Richard could voice the quick retort that formed in his mind, something caused him to pause. In a flash, he saw the Saturday spent working in Mom's new office from an eight-year-old's point of view.

With newfound compassion he responded to his son, "John, I know that Saturday is just about the most important day of the week when you're eight. I appreciate so much your willingness to give up your Saturday to help us get Mom's office decorated. It has been a very long day, and I bet you're tired too. But, I would like to show you how much I appreciate your support by stopping by the video store on the way home, so we can rent a family movie of your choice. What do ya say?"

In response to Dad's caring attitude, John's anguish and despair turned to pride, and he quietly said, "You're welcome, Dad. I would like that."

Sometimes, when we listen with our heart and not our ears, love wins and relationships flourish. For as Johann Wolfgang von Goethe says, "Correction does much, but encouragement does more."

POWER CAN DO BY GENTLENESS WHAT
VIOLENCE FAILS TO ACCOMPLISH.

LATIN PROVERB

CLINGING VINES

Scuppernong vines are parasites that grow up the trunks of and cling to healthy, firmly rooted trees in the southern United States. This walnut sized, dark skinned wild grape is used to make jams and jellies, and some Southerners use the hull skins for cobbler pies. The fruit produced by these vines has served as an inexpensive treat to poor families in the South for many years. In recent years scuppernongs have become more popular and can be purchased at stores all over the South.

"I AM THE VINE, YOU ARE THE BRANCHES; HE WHO ABIDES IN ME, AND I IN HIM, HE BEARS MUCH FRUIT, FOR APART FROM ME YOU CAN DO NOTHING."

JOHN 15:5 NASB

As beautiful, diverse, and tasty as the scuppernong is, it cannot survive on its own. It needs the life support of well-established trees to cling to and draw its nourishment from. Should the scuppernong vine be pulled away from its host tree, it would dry up and stop producing fruit.

Like the scuppernong, we cannot survive without total dependency on God. Without Him, we have no true life source, no lifeline, no nourishment, and we cannot produce good fruit.

We can, however, learn to cling to the Lord by surrendering ourselves to Him. We can draw nourishment through Bible study, prayer, worship, service, and heartfelt obedience. Like the scuppernong, clinging to our Source will help us grow healthy and produce much good fruit.

ALL WE WANT IN CHRIST, WE SHALL
FIND IN CHRIST. IF WE WANT LITTLE,
WE SHALL FIND LITTLE. IF WE WANT
MUCH, WE SHALL FIND MUCH;
BUT IF, IN UTTER HELPLESSNESS, WE
CAST OUR ALL ON CHRIST, HE WILL BE
TO US THE WHOLE TREASURY OF GOD.

HENRY BENJAMIN WHIPPLE

THE TWELVE DAYS
OF GIVING

"FREELY YOU HAVE RECEIVED,
FREELY GIVE."

MATTHEW 10:8

Patricia Moss listened to her children whine and cry in the toy department over which toy they'd get at Christmas and watched the pushing and shoving of the department store crowds. Then she stepped back for a minute to examine her family's values.

She decided to adopt a friend's tradition originating from the song, "The Twelve Days of Christmas." Beginning early in the fall, she would pick a family that needed encouragement to get into the Christmas spirit. Then twelve days before Christmas, she and her family would begin slipping anonymous gifts onto the front porch of that family. They would write cute poems to go with the gifts, such as, "Twelve days before Christmas, a true friend gave to me, twelve candy canes, to hang upon the tree." The eleventh day before Christmas might be eleven fancy bows, the tenth day, a "tin" of ten giant homemade cookies, on and on right up to Christmas Day.

One year the Moss family chose an elderly man who had suffered a stroke. He and his wife had decided not to put up a tree that year until the "twelve days" gifts started arriving. Another year they selected two families to cheer because both of the Moss brothers had friends whose families needed their love and care.

Patricia said that even after her sons were grown and had moved away, they still participated in this tradition when they returned home for Christmas.[44]

Patricia taught her children well, allowing them a hands-on opportunity not only to *see* good, but also to *do* good, moving them beyond their own problems as they gave generously of themselves to others.

HE THAT DOES GOOD
TO ANOTHER DOES
GOOD TO HIMSELF.

LUCIUS ANNAEUS SENECA

Is There Room?

In some places at Christmas, people place lanterns, or *farolitos,* along walls and paths or flat adobe roofs. Candles are set in sand inside paper bags and symbolize the journey of Joseph and Mary. These lanterns help the couple in their search for an empty room and reflect the starry light of Bethlehem that welcomed the Christ child's birth.

> SHE WRAPPED
> HIM IN CLOTHS
> AND PLACED
> HIM IN A
> MANGER,
> BECAUSE THERE
> WAS NO ROOM
> FOR THEM IN
> THE INN.
>
> LUKE 2:7

Reverend Douglas Showalter remembered the story of Mary and Joseph's search in a profound way one Christmas. In their white-steepled New England church, his parishioners always looked forward to the Christmas Eve service each year. In the dim auditorium, a group of young people fully presented the Nativity tableau.

This particular year, Reverend Showalter's church council realized Christmas Eve fell on the same night as the Alcoholics Anonymous large public meeting in their church fellowship hall. Would there be enough parking space? Would the AA group even attend, or would they want to spend the night with friends and family? Ultimately, the church leaders decided to let the AA group meet, regardless of the inconvenience.

The church parking lot overflowed as both AA and church members arrived. In the restroom that night, the reverend overheard a stranger—a young, sad-eyed teenage boy—talking to an older man: "I'm glad there's a meeting tonight. It's Christmas Eve, and I didn't have anywhere else to go." The older man from AA agreed.

The reverend watched the Nativity scene that night with a lump in his throat, grateful they had kept their "Inn" open to the ones who needed it.[45]

Our lives are like lanterns lighting the way to hope. When others come to us, looking for a safe place to shelter their hearts, will we cry "no room," or will we keep our doors open to all who need the Savior's love?

WHEN THERE IS ROOM IN THE HEART
THERE IS ROOM IN THE HOUSE.

DANISH PROVERB

THE "TO BE" LIST

Nearly all of us face our days with a to do list. The Scriptures compel us, however, to have a "to be" list.

While it may be important to accomplish certain tasks, engage in certain projects, or have certain encounters during a day, what is more important *for eternity* is the person we *are* throughout the day.

WHEN THE HOLY SPIRIT CONTROLS OUR LIVES HE WILL PRODUCE THIS KIND OF FRUIT IN US: LOVE, JOY, PEACE, PATIENCE, KINDNESS, GOODNESS, FAITHFULNESS, GENTLENESS AND SELF-CONTROL.

GALATIANS 5:22-23 TLB

From a to-do perspective, we tend to come before the Lord and say, "This is my list and this is my schedule. Please be with me, help me, and bless me."

From a to-be perspective, we might make these requests of the Lord:

- Help me to reflect Your love today.
- Help me to display Your joy.
- Help me to manifest Your peace.
- Help me to practice Your patience.
- Help me to express Your kindness.
- Help me to make known Your goodness.

- Help me to reveal Your faithfulness.
- Help me to show Your gentleness.
- Help me to exhibit Your self-control.

Wishful thinking does not produce these traits, however. They come from a life lived in communication with the Lord. They are the distinguishing marks of His presence in our lives. Our to-be list, therefore, must always begin with an invitation to the Holy Spirit to inspire us and impel us toward good works.

In order to *express* the Lord's kindness, for example, we first must see ourselves as *receiving* the Lord's kindness. In receiving His kindness, we become much more attuned to opportunities to show His kindness to others. The way we do our chores, hold our meetings, run our errands, and teach in our classrooms are opportunities to show His kindness to those around us.

When we make our to-be list our top priority, the things we have to do become much more obvious—and far less burdensome!

BREATHE ON ME, BREATH OF GOD;
FILL ME WITH LIFE ANEW, THAT I MAY
LOVE WHAT THOU DOST LOVE, AND
DO WHAT THOU WOULDST DO.

EDWIN HATCH

MISPLACED EXPECTATIONS

GIVE THANKS IN ALL
CIRCUMSTANCES, FOR THIS IS GOD'S
WILL FOR YOU IN CHRIST JESUS.

1 THESSALONIANS 5:18

Most of us at some time indulge in the endless chase for perfection in our lives: perfect home, perfect job, no conflicts. And most of us discover quickly the futility of such expectations.

Every year *Dear Abby* prints a familiar story written by Emily Kingsley called, "Welcome to Holland." Emily, a writer, lecturer, and talented mother of an adult child with Down syndrome, knows about expectations. Others have asked her what it's like raising a child with disabilities. In her story, Emily uses a metaphor. She compares the expectation of a child's birth to planning a vacation trip to Italy. She mentions the joy of deciding on tourist spots to visit and the anticipation of all the sights you would see upon your arrival.

She then describes the scenario upon landing in your vacation spot. Surely a mistake has been made, because the stewardess on your plane welcomes you not to Italy, but to Holland. You argue, but nothing changes. You are in Holland, and there you will stay.

Anyone who has ever been to Holland knows that tulips, windmills, and Rembrandts make Holland a beautiful place. Emily points out that it's just not what you expected. You *planned* on going to Italy.

In her poignant illustration, Kingsley challenges the reader to focus not on unmet expectations (Italy), but on the beauty of where you are (Holland).

When life doesn't turn out perfectly—the way we planned—we have a choice. Whether it's as minor as a holiday gone awry or as major as a prince charming that turned into an ugly frog, God wants us to celebrate that "very special, very lovely thing" about our circumstance.

NOTHING WITH GOD
CAN BE ACCIDENTAL

HENRY WADSWORTH LONGFELLOW

Good News

Christmas letters. They come every December if the author is well prepared. Some don't arrive until late January. Those come from the harried and hurried whose lives were just too complicated in late fall to do anything different. But whenever they arrive, they are welcome.

They may be tucked into a greeting card or accompanied by a snapshot. They may come all alone, in their own envelope, bearing their own cancelled stamp. They may be handwritten, computer processed, or churned out by a copy machine. But however they are delivered, they are treasured.

Some fill only one sheet; others ramble on for pages. Some are candid and humorous; others bring concerns and sadness. But all are filled with a common element. All bring news from far away.

> GOOD NEWS FROM FAR AWAY IS LIKE COLD WATER TO THE THIRSTY.
>
> PROVERBS 25:25 TLB

Christmas letters. We've all come to expect them each year. That letter may be the only opportunity we have to reconnect with acquaintances and catch up on their family's happenings.

But Christmas letters can be more than newsletters about friends' activities. One woman takes the

Christmas letters she receives and divides them into four piles, setting one pile aside for each quarter of the year. During that three-month period, she prays for the authors of those letters and, as time permits, even pens a quick note to say hello. In this way, the Christmas letters she receives each year bring her good news but also bring the sender her thoughts and prayers. Her simple gesture creates a refreshing circle of love.

What will you do with your Christmas letters this year?

LIFE IS THE FLOWER OF WHICH
LOVE IS THE HONEY.

VICTOR HUGO

REFERENCES

ENDNOTES

1. *Spiritual Fitness,* Doris Donnelly (San Francisco: Harper, 1993), pp. 111-124.

2. *Knight's Master Book of 4,000 Illustrations,* Walter B. Knight, (Grand Rapids, MI: William B. Eerdmans Publishing Co., 1956), p. 71.

3. *Macartney's Illustrations,* Clarence E. Macartney (NY: Abingdon Press, 1945, 1946), pp. 19, 172.

4. *Newsweek,* February 15, 1999, p. 47.

5. The Misheard Lyrics Website, www.kissthisguy.com.

6. *Today in the Word,* September 2, 1992.

7. Maya Angelou, *Wouldn't Take Nothin' for My Journey Now* (N.Y.:, Random House, 1993), p. 62.

8. Judy Seymour, "The Freeway Not Taken: Lake Route Worth the Slower Pace," *Minneapolis Star Tribune,* 05-12-1997, p. 15A.

9. *Reader's Digest,* October 1991, p. 61.

10. Charles R. Swindoll, *Hand Me Another Brick* (Nashville, TN: Thomas Nelson, 1978), pp. 82, 88.

11. Author Unknown.

12. "The Endless Streetcar Ride into the Night, and the Tinfoil Noose," Jean Shepherd, in *The Riverside Reader,* Vol. 1, (Boston, MA: Houghton Mifflin Company, 1985), p. 32.

13. Meryle Secrest, *Leonard Bernstein: A Life,* (Knopf, 1995).

14. Common Ground, January 1990.

15. *Teaching and Learning in Communities of Faith,* Linda J. Vogel, (San Francisco, CA: Jossey-Bass Publishers, 1991), p. 124.

16. Mier, Paul, M.D., "Confessions of a Workaholic," *The Physician,* March/April 1990.

[17] Nanette Thorsen-Snipes. Adapted from *Power for Living*, April 1992.

[18] *The New Dictionary of Thoughts*, Tryon Edwards, ed. (NY: Standard Book Company, 1963), p. 506.

[19] *The Man Who Talks with the Flowers*, Glenn Clark (St. Paul: Macalester Park Publishing Co., 1939), pp. 17, 21-22.

[20] *Book of Prayers*, Robert Van de Weyer, ed. (NY: Harper Collins, 1993), p. 67.

[21] *The Finishing Touch*, Charles R. Swindoll, (Dallas: Word Publishing, 1994), p. 274.

[22] *The Joy of Working*, Denis Waitley and Reni L. Witt (NY: Dodd, Mead and Company, 1985), pp. 722-723.

[23] Ibid, pp. 23-24.

[24] *The Finishing Touch*, Swindoll, pp. 186-187.

[25] *Unto the Hills: A Devotional Treasury*, Billy Graham, (Waco, TX: Word Books, 1986), p. 158.

[26] *A Moment a Day*, Mary Beckwith and Kathi Mills, ed. (Ventura, CA: Regal Books, 1988), p. 25.

[27] Ibid, p. 174.

[28] Ibid, p. 184.

[29] *Encyclopedia of 7,700 Illustrations*, Paul Lee Tan (Garland, TX: Bible Communications, Inc., 1979), p. 1,387.

[30] *Give Your Life a Lift*, Herman W. Gockel (St. Louis: Concordia Publishing House, 1968), pp. 38-39.

[31] *Reader's Digest*, April 1996, p. 116.

[32] *Encyclopedia of 7,700 Illustrations*, Tan, pp. 1,477-1,479.

[33] *Psychology Today*, November/December 1994, p. 16.

[34] *Encyclopedia of 7,700 Illustrations*, Tan, p. 1,477.

[35] *Teatime by the Tea Ambassador*, Aubrey Franklin (NY: Frederick Fell Publishers, Inc., 1981), p. 62.

36 *The Treasury of Inspirational Anecdotes, Quotations & Illustrations,* E. Paul Hovey (Grand Rapids, MI: Fleming H. Revell [Baker Books], 1994), pp. 204-205.

37 *Thesaurus of Anecdotes,* Edmund Fuller, ed. (NY: The Wise Book Co., 1945), p. 103.

38 *Tales of the Shimmering Sky,* Susan Milord (Charlotte, VT: Williamson Publishing, 1996), p. 47.

39 *The Best-Loved Poems of the American People,* Selected by Hazel Felleman (New York: Doubleday, 1936), p. 305.

40 Author Unknown. Adapted from *Story Page for Teachers,* www.geocities.com, March 12, 1998. Quotation by William H. Danforth.

41 *He Cares, He Comforts,* Corrie ten Boom (Old Tappan, NJ: Fleming H. Revell, 1977), pp. 29-33.

42 *You Can Win with Love,* Dale E. Galloway, (Irvine: Harvest House, 1976).

43 Steven Ger, "The Undying Flame," *Kindred Spirit* (Winter 1999).

44 *Dallas Morning News* (February 2, 1992), pp. 72-73.

45 Rev. Douglas Showalter, "Nowhere Else to Go," www.heart-warmers.com, 21 December 1999, http://dispatch.mail-list.com/archives/heartwawrmers/msg00490.html.

Additional copies of this book and other titles
in the *Quiet Moments with God Devotional* series
are available from your local bookstore.

Quiet Moments with God

Quiet Moments with God for Couples

Quiet Moments with God for Mothers

Quiet Moments with God for Women

If you have enjoyed this book,
or if it has impacted your life,
we would like to hear from you.
Please contact us at:

Honor Books

Department E

P.O. Box 55388

Tulsa, Oklahoma 74155

Or, by e-mail at *info@honorbooks.com*